2nd edition, revised and expanded

What's in a Name?
A Young Person's Jewish Genealogy Workbook

STEPHEN M. COHEN ✡ CARYN ALTER

A Publication of JewishGen
Edmond J. Safra Plaza, 36 Battery Place, New York, NY 10280
646.494.2972 | info@JewishGen.org | www.jewishgen.org

JewishGen is the Genealogical Research Division of the
Museum of Jewish Heritage – A Living Memorial to the Holocaust

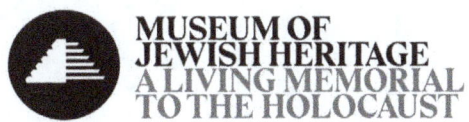

What's in a Name?
A Young Person's Jewish Genealogy Workbook

Copyright © 2024 by Stephen M. Cohen and Caryn Alter. All rights reserved.

First published by Hadassa Word Press, an imprint of OmniScriptum GmbH & Co. KG, in 2017

Second Edition: Published by JewishGen July 2024, Tammuz 5784

Authors, layout, and cover design: Stephen M. Cohen and Caryn Alter

This book may not be reproduced, in whole or in part, including illustrations in any form (beyond that copying permitted by Sections 107 and 108 of the U.S. Copyright Law and except by reviewers for public press), without written permission from the publisher.

JewishGen Press is not responsible for inaccuracies or omissions in the original work and makes no representations regarding the accuracy of this work.

ISBN: 978-1-962054-00-3 (hard cover: 154 pages, alk. paper)

About JewishGen.org

JewishGen, an affiliate of the Museum of Jewish Heritage - A Living Memorial to the Holocaust, serves as the global home for Jewish genealogy. Featuring unparalleled access to 30+ million records, it offers unique search tools, along with opportunities for researchers to connect with others who share similar interests. Award winning resources such as the Family Finder, Discussion Groups, and ViewMate, are relied upon by thousands each day.

In addition, JewishGen's extensive informational, educational and historical offerings, such as the Jewish Communities Database, Yizkor Book translations, InfoFiles, Family Tree of the Jewish People, and KehilaLinks, provide critical insights, first-hand accounts, and context about Jewish communal and familial life throughout the world.

Offered as a free resource, JewishGen.org has facilitated thousands of family connections and success stories, and is currently engaged in an intensive expansion effort that will bring many more records, tools, and resources to its collections.

Please visit https://www.jewishgen.org/ to learn more.

Executive Director: **Avraham Groll**

About JewishGen Press

JewishGen Press (formerly the Yizkor Books-in-Print Project) is the publishing division of JewishGen.org, and provides a venue for the publication of non-fiction books pertaining to Jewish genealogy, history, culture, and heritage.

In addition to the Yizkor Book category, publications in the Other Non-Fiction category include Shoah memoirs and research, genealogical research, collections of genealogical and historical materials, biographies, diaries and letters, studies of Jewish experience and cultural life in the past, academic theses, and other books of interest to the Jewish community.

Please visit https://www.jewishgen.org/Yizkor/ybip.html to learn more.

Director of JewishGen Press: Joel Alpert
Managing Editor - Jessica Feinstein
Publications Manager - Susan Rosin

Praise for
What's in a Name? A Young Person's Jewish Genealogy Workbook

What's in a Name? A Young Person's Jewish Genealogy Workbook is a much needed and invaluable resource for any student wishing to embark on studying the field of Jewish genealogy—a must in any educator's library, too!

—Eli Rabinowitz, Director, International Association of Jewish Genealogical Societies; WE ARE HERE! Foundation & IN MY POCKET Project

For young genealogists, just getting started can be overwhelming; this book changes the playing field for them. As a student text, the format is easily digestible for middle and high school students. It is a comprehensive tool which includes strategies, historical information relative to researching Jewish roots and actual worksheet pages on which students can record their data. *What's in a Name? A Young Person's Jewish Genealogy Workbook* should be a new addition to every family library!

—Felicia Mode Alexander, President, Jewish Genealogical and Archival Society of Greater Philadelphia

I recommend this book as a valuable resource guide for anyone interested in getting started in their genealogical research or as a gift for any person of any age that has any interest or curiosity about their own family history.

—Lew Meixler, Former Chair of the Mercer County Jewish Genealogy Society at Beth El Synagogue (East Windsor, New Jersey)

I am very impressed with this comprehensive book the authors have written. I have been doing genealogy for many years and I can't think of anything else I would have included. Although written for young people I would highly recommend this for any beginner.

—Susan Kobren, Past President, Jewish Genealogical Society of North Jersey

This Jewish genealogy workbook is a treasure trove of resources for young people, that can motivate them to learn about their families by exploring "secret codes, history, genetics and science." … The authors have made a complex topic easily accessible through their clear and informal style.

—Marge Kaplan, Jewish Book Council (on book's first edition)

In memory of my mother, Elaine Feder ז״ל, who instilled in me a love of family.
In memory of my father, Earl Feder ז״ל, who instilled in me a love of history.
With abounding love and appreciation for my own family—together we are creating our own history.

—Caryn Alter

To all my family members, both living and deceased, who have helped me and attempted to answer my incessant questions, *tsu mayne kinder, Denele un Khanele, vos meynen az ikh ver a kleyn bisl meshuge vegn genealogye,* to Naomi, who has graciously tolerated my erstwhile obsession, and to my parents, Paul ז״ל and Brenda Cohen, who always supported my fascination with genealogy with interest and assistance, but especially to my mother, who first taught me at age seven how to draw a descendant chart.

—Stephen M. Cohen

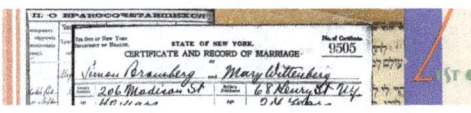

Juliet:
"What's in a name? That which we call a rose
By any other name would smell as sweet."
                —William Shakespeare, *Romeo and Juliet* (2.2.1–2)

Contents

Forward xiii
Prefaces xv
Acknowledgements xvii

Introduction xix
What's in a Name?   xix
To Parents   xix
To Educators   xx
To Genealogists   xx

Why Do Genealogy? 1
It's Useful   1
It's Worthwhile   1
It's Fun   3
It's a Mitzvah   3

Genealogy Techniques 5
What to Record   5
Descendant Charts and Ancestry Charts   6
Interviews   8
Finding History in Your Home   9
You Are What You Eat   13
Start Your Engines—Search Engines, That Is!   15
DNA Testing   15
Recording Your Sources   17

The Name Game 19
Ancient Names   19
Talmudic Names   19
Medieval Names   19
Nicknames   20
Names and Dialects   20
Jews' Clues   21
Baby-Naming Customs   23

You and Your Family 25
Write What You Know   25
Genealogy and Math   28
Ask Your Relatives to Add More   29
Visit and Do a Mitzvah   30

Watch Your Words 31
Hebrew   31

Aramaic   32
Yiddish   32
Ladino   33
Russian   33
Fraktur   34
Kurrent and *Sütterlin*   **34**

Go Back in Time 37
Census Records   37
Death Certificates   40
Birth Certificates   40
Marriage Certificates   41
City and Telephone Directories   42
Professional Directories   43
Yearbooks and Autograph Books   43
Military Records   44
Social Security Records   46
Probate Documents   46
Patents   47
Newspapers   47

Mysteries in the Cemetery.. 49
What's on a Gravestone?   49
A Real Example   49
Let's Decode Some Symbols   50
The Grave on the Right   50
Myth-Busting Alert!!   51
The Grave on the Left   51
Become a Decoding Detective!   51
Some Other Symbols on Gravestones   54
More Things to Learn from Gravestones   54
The Weird Hebrew Letter   55
Landsmanshaftn and Mutual Aid Societies   55
Be Respectful at the Cemetery   57
Finding the Cemetery   57
Decode a Relative's Gravestone!   58

Clues from Beyond the United States 59
British Commonwealth   59
Continental Europe   63
Latin America   66

Across the Ocean: Your Own Voyage of Discovery. 69
Arriving in "The Golden Land"   69
Leaving the "Old Country"   70

So How Do I Find These Records?   71
Myth-Busting Alert!! Myth-Busting Alert!!   71
Schwartz or Szwarc? A Spelling Lesson   72
A Name Puzzle   73
Other Emigration Records   77
Detention of Immigrants   78
Passports   78

The "Old Country" 81
Where Jews Lived in Eastern Europe   81
Where Jews Lived in the Mediterranean Basin   82
Jews in Other Lands   82
Kahal Records and Civil Records   83
Census Records in the "Old Country"   85
Telephone Books   86
Business Directories   86
Tax and Voter Records   86
Ketubot   88
Newspapers   90
Military records   90
Cemeteries   91

Remnants of a Community: The Holocaust.............. 93
Yizkor Books   93
Yad Vashem Records   94
Other Holocaust Museums, Memorials, and Archives   95
Interviews with Family Members   95
Survivors' Published Accounts   95

Digging Up Clues from the Land of Israel 97
Aliyah   97
Military Records   98
Cemeteries and Burial Records   98
Lists of People   99
Telephone Directories   99
Genealogy Societies in Israel   99

Beneath the Surface 101
Conversion (or Not)   101
Adoption   102
Criminals in Your Past   102
Multiple Marriages and Divorce   103
The Holocaust   105
Be Considerate   105

What Do I Do with It All? 107
Digital Storage   107
Storing Paper   107
Storing Photographs   108
Movies, Slides, and Negatives   109
Videotapes and Audio Tapes   109
Vinyl Records   110
Other Objects   110
Be the Archivist!   110

Where Do I Go from Here? 111
Meet Other Genealogists   111
Tell Your Relatives   111
Register at JewishGen   111
Attend a Conference   112
Submit a Page of Testimony   112
Take Stock of Your Work   112
Lekh L'kha (Go Forth)   112

Continuing the Journey 113
What's in a Name?   113

Appendix: Resources for Research 115
Books   115
Websites to Try   116

Words to Know 123

✡ Forward

What's in a Name? A Young Person's Jewish Genealogy Workbook by Stephen M. Cohen and Caryn Alter is a highly readable how-to book for young people interested in researching their Jewish family history. Each chapter is full of helpful information designed to engage the next generation in our fascinating and addictive hobby.

After four decades as a genealogist and history teacher, I can testify that the task of combing through records can be daunting, especially without any guidance. But today, with the widespread use of DNA testing and genealogy websites, conducting research is much easier and fun for all ages!

For young genealogists, just getting started can be overwhelming; this book changes the playing field for them. As a student text, the format is easily digestible for middle and high school students. It is a comprehensive tool which includes strategies, historical information related to researching Jewish roots, and actual worksheet pages on which students can record their data.

What's in a Name? A Young Person's Jewish Genealogy Workbook should be a new addition to every family library!

Felicia Mode Alexander
President, Jewish Genealogical and Archival Society of Greater Philadelphia

✡ Preface to the Second Edition

The Internet truly launched the "Golden Age of Genealogy." Although new and different websites and resources appear, and older ones vanish, the amount of information available to today's genealogists continues to increase at a lightning-fast pace.

Even the genealogical knowledge of this book's authors has evolved in the years since the first edition of this book was published. Our quest, with this new edition, is to offer the next generation of "genealogical detectives" information that is as current and understandable as possible, and to impart to them the sense of excitement we have whenever we discover a new piece of our heritage. To that end, the second edition includes new chapters about Jewish naming traditions and the myriad of languages that are important for Jewish genealogy research, as well as an expanded Appendix.

All items shown in this book's images are from the authors' collections unless otherwise indicated.

✡ Preface to the First Edition

This book began with a discussion between its two authors in 2010. The authors, founding members of their synagogue's Jewish genealogy club, talked about developing some type of family history project for their synagogue's religious school students. They subsequently did an online search for Jewish genealogy books geared toward young adults, and found nothing that was current. From that initial discussion and literature search, the seeds of this workbook were planted. And, as they say, "the rest is history."

In this workbook, we use the spelling standards and guidelines of the YIVO Institute for Jewish Research to represent most Yiddish words used in the text. We have written the workbook with the assumption that the reader has at least a basic knowledge of Jewish terms (e.g., *brit milah*, *mitzvah*, *challah*). Although a familiarity with elementary Hebrew or the Hebrew alphabet is helpful, it is not required to understand the concepts in this book.

Genealogy is now largely done through the Internet via searches of the numerous websites, databases, and digital archives that are currently available. However, nothing in the world of genealogy remains constant, and even up to the last revisions of this manuscript, we were adding information about newly created online resources. We therefore sincerely apologize if any of the resources we listed have changed or been discontinued since the publication of this book.

Psychologist Marshall Duke found, through his research[1] at Emory University, that "family stories provide a sense of identity through time, and help children understand who they are in the world." His research also showed that teenagers who knew more stories about their families exhibited "higher levels of emotional well-being…."

It is our hope that this workbook will help its readers discover their own family stories and, in so doing, create for them a sense of identity that will last a lifetime.

---

[1] Robyn Fivush, Jennifer G. Bohanek, and Marshall Duke, "The Intergenerational Self: Subjective Perspective and Family History," in *Individual and Collective Self-Continuity*, ed. F. Sani (Mahwah, NJ: Erlbaum, 2008).

✡ Acknowledgements

A workbook that attempts to cover the dizzying array of topics that encompass the field of Jewish genealogy, especially a workbook designed for junior genealogists, requires the knowledge and input of more than just its authors. Therefore, we wish to express our gratitude to many people who generously gave their time and advice, and offered materials for illustrative purposes.

We thank Dr. Mara W. Cohen Ioannides for information on Sephardim, Jacques Berny for insights into French genealogy, and Avraham Greenhaus ז״ל for help with the interpretation of gravestones. Sincere thanks also go to Pavla (Kosta) Alter, Barbara Pollack, Martin Potasnick, Dr. Pascal Renault, Nikki Spencer, Ray Sylvester, Frank Vigon, and Zohar Yereslav, who provided many of the images you see in this book. We thank Dr. Naomi Basickes and Sandy Basickes ז״ל for sharing with us an old family recipe, William Beitmann for providing terminology on German-Jewish cuisine and a sample of *Kurrent* handwriting, Francine Safir for providing a sample of *Sütterlin* handwriting, Sasha Cohen Ioannides for explaining teen vocabulary, and Donald J. Cox, Jr., Esq. for offering expert guidance concerning copyright. We are also grateful to Roz Blanck for providing information about the David-Horodoker Organization.

Modern Jewish genealogy would not exist without the Internet. We are most grateful to Dr. Stephen P. Morse for allowing screenshots of his "One-Step Webpages" website in our chapter about finding relatives who emigrated through Ellis Island. Our sincere thanks to the Statue of Liberty—Ellis Island Foundation, Inc. for permission to use its images of ship manifests. Sincere gratitude to Yad Vashem – The World Holocaust Remembrance Center, for allowing us to use images of personal records and Pages of Testimony from its Central Database of Shoah Victims' Names.

Once the basic manuscript was complete, we asked reviewers to assess the book. We are indebted to the following reviewers of both the first and second editions for providing helpful comments and suggestions concerning content, grammar, style, and layout: Felicia Mode Alexander, Dr. James Brazell, Kathy Brazell, Hannah Cohen, Susan Kobren, Leslie Kornsgold, Lew Meixler, Eli Rabinowitz, and Dr. Nathan Reiss.

We are grateful to Lew Meixler and the members of Beth El Synagogue's Jewish Genealogy Club (now the Mercer County Jewish Genealogy Society at Beth El Synagogue), in East Windsor, New Jersey, who steadfastly provided us with support, inspiration, and information as our project took shape—for both the first and second editions.

And we thank all our family members and friends who have contributed—in ways big and small—to our genealogical journeys over the years. Although not all their contributions could be included in this book, we appreciated them greatly. We thank them for their patience as they endured a barrage of occasionally quirky questions as we sought the "Next Big Genealogical Breakthrough."

Last, but certainly not least, we are most grateful to Jessica Feinstein, Managing Editor of JewishGen Press: It was her vision that gave us the opportunity to share the second edition of this workbook with the world. *Todah rabah*, Jessica!

 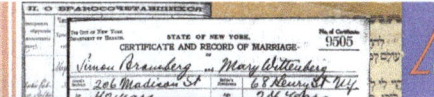  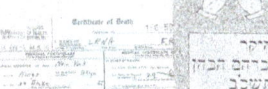

Introduction

✡ *What's in a Name?*

A NAME IS MORE than just the word that our parents or our friends use when they want to get our attention. Our first, middle, and last names can represent a link to our families and to our past.

By being a "Jewish genealogy detective," you can try to solve mysteries and piece together tidbits of your family story. Soon your ancestors will come to life. Every life has many stories if you just look hard enough. Unearthing these stories is like finding hidden treasure!

Knowing our past is a gift we give to future generations. As you read this Jewish genealogy workbook and fill in the different sections, we hope that your past comes alive. May your journey through history be as exciting and meaningful as our journeys!

Happy Hunting!

Photograph restored by Stephen M. Cohen

✡ *To Parents*

When parents name a child, often they are creating a legacy that connects their child to their ancestors. Parents who explain to their children the meaning or significance of their English and Jewish names are giving them the gift of belonging—to a family, a culture, a religion, a nationality. Different countries and cultures have different traditions for naming their children. Some of these traditions will be explored later in this workbook.

Please be aware that answering a child's questions about family history can sometimes require sensitivity on the part of the parents. You will need to determine how much of this information to share with your child at this time. The popularity of testing DNA to discover one's ancestry can often overshadow more traditional—but usually more effective—genealogical research methods. In this book, we prefer to focus on a "detective-based approach" to studying genealogy.

Additionally, although the amount of free online information related to genealogy has exploded in recent years, there may still be some costs involved in genealogy research. Obtaining copies of certain documents, joining a genealogy society, and subscribing to an online database may cost money. Materials such as archival-quality page holders and photo storage boxes may be worthwhile to purchase. These topics will be discussed in more detail in this workbook.

✡ To Educators

Teachers who encourage their students to study their family histories give them the tools to create an identity for themselves. Genealogical research can stimulate an interest in complementary fields such as history, geography, foreign languages, and other subjects. A discussion about digitizing old audio tapes and videotapes could even spark interest in budding multimedia engineers. This book will also serve as a springboard for activities that will help students write their own personal stories that they can one day share with their families.

We have included in the "Words to Know" section a short list of the Jewish genealogical terms introduced in this workbook, thus enabling your students to enrich their vocabularies.

✡ To Genealogists

This workbook is an overview of the world of Jewish genealogy. We cannot include every possible detail about research, but we do hope to instill in our readers a love for their heritage, and the motivation to find a local Jewish genealogy club for additional guidance. While we have done our best to provide a thorough introduction to Jewish genealogy for young people within the pages of this book, we realize that we could not possibly cover every topic relevant to this field of study. We hope that our book will inspire further genealogy pursuits by its readers.

We strived to give readers an overview of the numerous resources available to them as they begin to document their past. Children are likely not aware of the wide variety of genealogical documents and tools available. Therefore, we felt it was important to define the terms we use throughout the workbook, as well as include examples from our own personal collections to illustrate ideas that are discussed in the various chapters.

Why Do Genealogy?

Do you like solving puzzles?
Do you like exploring mysteries?
Do you like secret codes?
Do you like learning history?
Do you like genetics and science?
Do you like folktales?

Well, genealogy is for you. Genealogy is the study of records or accounts of the ancestry and heritage of a person, family, or group. Perhaps stories about great-grandma escaping Eastern Europe, or Uncle David reading the Haggadah at the Passover Seder, have captured your attention. Perhaps you've heard no stories, but uncovering some by yourself seems worthwhile. We genealogists know how much fun researching our family histories can be, but sometimes the relatives just don't get why it's cool. Here are some snappy reasons to give Mom, Dad, or grumpy Aunt Helen when they wonder why you are asking them all sorts of nosy questions.

✡ It's Useful

There are many different traits that we can inherit from our parents and grandparents. These traits can include characteristics like blue eyes, red hair, dimples, or food allergies. Certain traits appear more often in specific population groups, including Jews.

It might be interesting for you to make the discovery that you and some of your relatives are left-handed or can sing well. You might even find out that twins run in your family!

Write down some inherited traits that you think may exist in your family.

✡ It's Worthwhile

History class in school may seem like a long list of names and dates to memorize that have no real connection to you or your family. When you study your own genealogy, you begin to understand why your great-grandparents migrated from Europe to North America, who Czar Nicholas II was and why he was important to the Jews, or why cousin Yitzhak lives on a kibbutz in Israel.

Geography starts to take on new meaning when you can discuss the "Old Country," a *shtetl* (small town) in Romania, or a village in Greece. Those fragile, old letters scrawled in what looks like Hebrew become important. Perhaps those letters are actually written in the Yiddish or Ladino languages, which you can learn—and can make your own secret language (more about these and other languages in the "Watch Your Words" chapter)! Maybe those letters tell of the *elter-zeyde* (great-grandfather) after whom you are named, and you can then discover why your parents thought it was important that he be remembered through you.

Your family was a part of history, and when you study your genealogy, you learn your own custom-made history, and how you fit into today's world.

In which country or countries did your ancestors live?

Front and back of a postcard from a relative of Caryn Alter's maternal grandfather. What languages are these? (Answer: Yiddish on the front; Russian on the back)

What language(s) do you think your ancestors spoke in their country of origin? In the left column, write the language. In the right column, name the alphabet (for example, Hebrew or Cyrillic [Russian]) that was used to write that language.

Language	Alphabet

✡ It's Fun

Some people like to collect trading cards or vinyl albums. Some like to collect rocks or stickers. Maybe you like dolls or souvenirs from around the world. Well, you can also collect relatives. You might be related to a politician or rabbi or Nobel Prize-winning scientist. Maybe your cousin is a rock musician or sculptor or famous doctor or lawyer. We have found, in our genealogy research, that often a particular family branch excels at a particular talent, like music, writing, or business. It's fun to figure out those connections.

Do you have any interesting or famous people in your family? List them here, along with what makes them famous.

Relative	How that relative is famous

✡ It's a Mitzvah

Family members are pleased when young people like you take an interest in their lives. Sit down with them, ask questions, and take notes. Often they have interesting stories to tell about themselves from when they were your age.

Why Do Genealogy?

Write down some questions that you would like to ask your relatives about your family.

Genealogy Techniques

When you learn to play guitar, you develop certain techniques for playing music. Likewise, becoming a good soccer player requires proper technique and teamwork. And winning a video game means you find an appropriate strategy to slip past the traps and gain extra points. In the same way, when doing genealogy research, it takes a bit of effort to organize and understand your findings.

✡ What to Record

When you find out facts about a relative, what should you write down about that person? That depends on what you'd like to know. Are you interested more in that person's history, or that person's relationship to you?

Most genealogists (people who study or trace family histories) agree that certain basic information is necessary to learn about a person's unique place in history. You should record:

- Date and place of birth
- Jewish name (for Jewish relatives)
- Date and place of marriage (if the person married)
- Where the person lives or has lived
- Date of migration (if the person moved from one country to another)
- Date and place of death (if the person is no longer alive)
- Cemetery where the person is buried (if the person is no longer alive)

Other information that might be fun or useful to record may include:

- Schools attended, degrees earned
- Job(s)
- Hobbies and interests
- Genetic traits, like red hair or dimples
- Any other fascinating facts, like prizes or honors the person received

Photo by Jennifer Burk on Unsplash

Pick one person from your family who's no longer alive, and find out some information about that person. Write the information in the table below. If you don't know an exact date, you can use the word "about" next to it. If you're not sure about a place, you can put a question mark after the place. If you have no idea at all about a fact, leave it blank, or write "unknown."

Family member's name	
Birth date	
Birthplace	
Jewish name (if the family member had one)	
Date and place of marriage (if the family member married)	
Places where this family member lived	
If the family member moved from one country to another, give the dates and places	
Date and place of death	
Name of the cemetery where family member is buried, and the town where it is located	
Any other interesting facts about that family member	

✦ Descendant Charts and Ancestry Charts

After you get past some initial information about your grandparents and first cousins, family research can get tricky. Genealogists have developed ways of organizing their family research into easy-to-understand formats.

One diagram that genealogists often use to display their family is called the *descendant chart*. A descendant chart starts with a pair of ancestors (say, two great-grandparents), and shows how all their descendants are connected to them and to one another.

Here is a very small example of a fictional descendant chart:

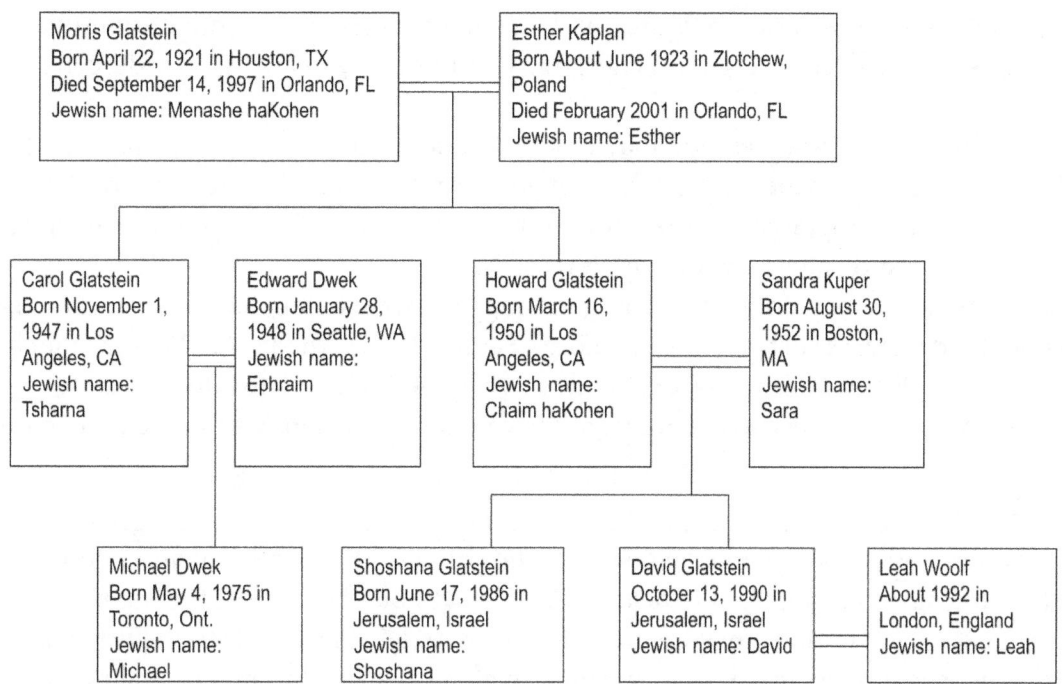

The double-line shows marriage between two people. You can see how easy it is to figure out who is related to whom from a descendant chart. This kind of chart is best for showing relationships among all your cousins in a particular branch of your family.

If you'd like to work backward in time from you to all your direct ancestors, you can build an *ancestry chart*. An ancestry chart starts with one person, and shows parents, grandparents, and so on, backward in time. Here is an example of a fictional ancestry chart:

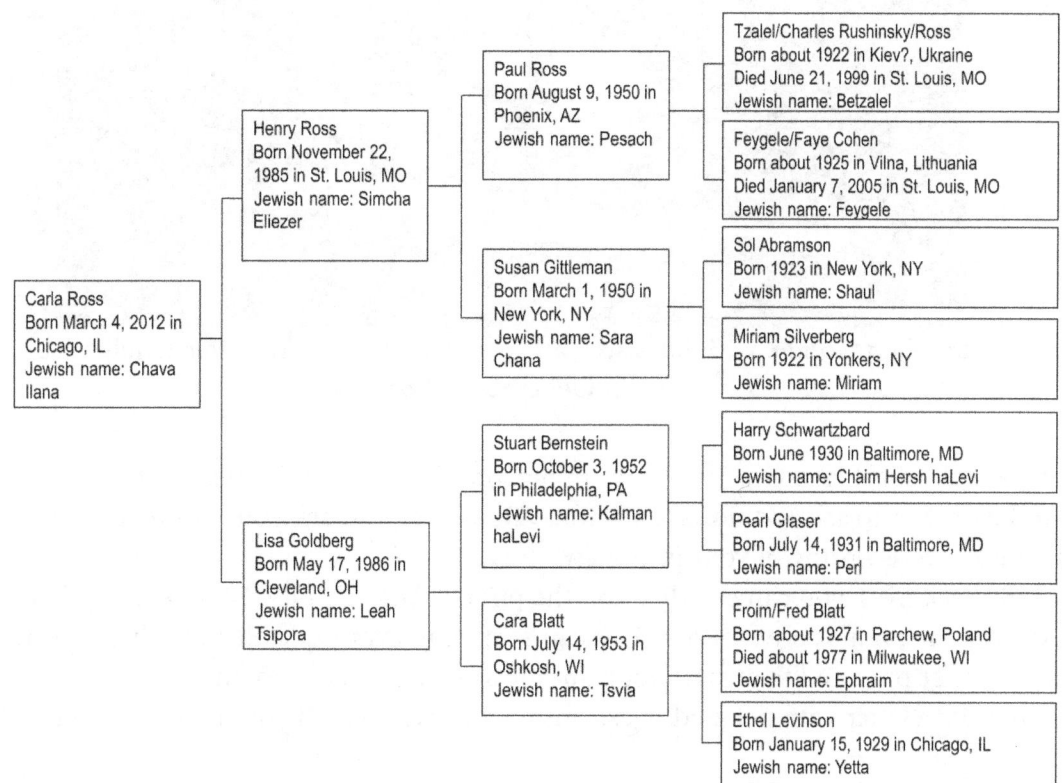

With this kind of chart, it's easier to figure out your direct ancestors. You might find this chart useful to track Jewish names that reappear every few generations, or to see if you are directly descended from rabbis, for instance.

After the first dozen or so relatives, you may find it hard to keep track of everyone. And drawing and redrawing charts on a sheet of paper can get tiring if you keep learning new facts. Therefore, most genealogists use special computer programs to record their information. Once the computer has the information, you can print out charts and enter new information easily.

You can purchase genealogy programs from genealogy software companies, or you can post your information on online databases such as jewishgen.org's Family Tree of the Jewish People, but check with a parent first. There are advantages and disadvantages to each method. Talk to a local genealogy club about which kinds of software or online choices are right for you. Most genealogy software costs money.

✡ Interviews

You see interviews of famous people on television or online all the time. Did you know that interviews are essential to learning about your family history? YOU get to play the role of the interviewer, and YOU have the power to ask the questions that are important to YOU. During your interview, you spend time with someone who may have not just important information about the family, but stories and wisdom to share as well.

Stephen Cohen, with his sister and great aunt, examine their family tree in December 1981

Whenever possible, it is best to do interviews in person. That way, you can see the other person's facial expressions, and it's easier to ask additional questions. Don't forget to ask your family member if you can make an audio or video recording of your interview.

If you can't visit relatives, you can call them on the phone. Although it might be difficult, try to take careful notes during the phone conversation. You can even email your questions to them ahead of time, so your relatives are better prepared to answer your questions when you call them.

You can also write a letter with detailed questions to your relatives. If you include a stamped, self-addressed envelope with your letter, it might improve your chances of getting back the answers to your questions.

If your relatives are comfortable with the world of digital devices, you can interview them via computer, smart phone, or tablet. There are now lots of ways to schedule virtual meetings with people. Use a screen-capture program to record the video or audio.

When you are finished with the interview, the person you interviewed would probably appreciate a summary of your notes. They will be impressed with all of your hard work and may even offer some corrections or additions to your notes.

✡ Finding History in Your Home

Believe it or not, your very own house can provide a treasure trove of clues about your family's past. Ask your parents if they have any of the following items in the house:

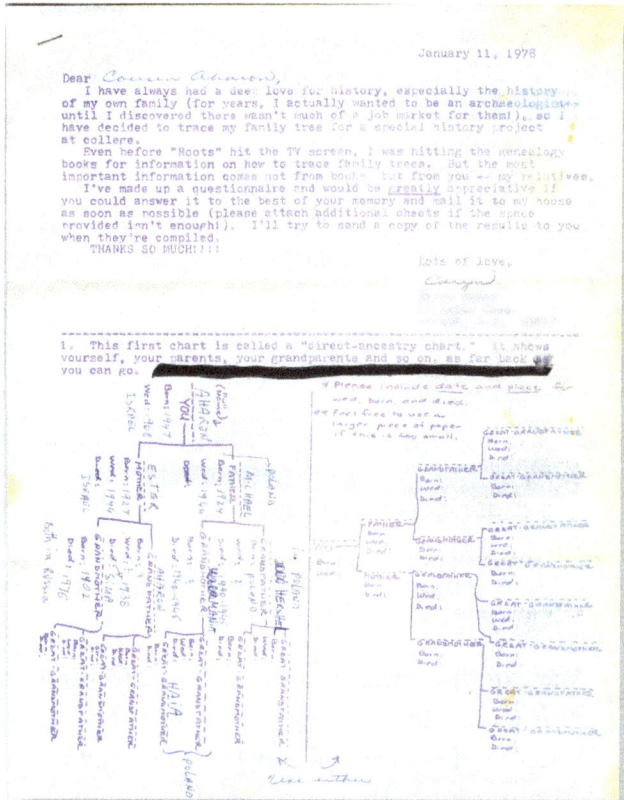

Questionnaire Caryn Alter mailed to her relatives when she started her genealogy quest

Go on a treasure hunt in your home with a parent!

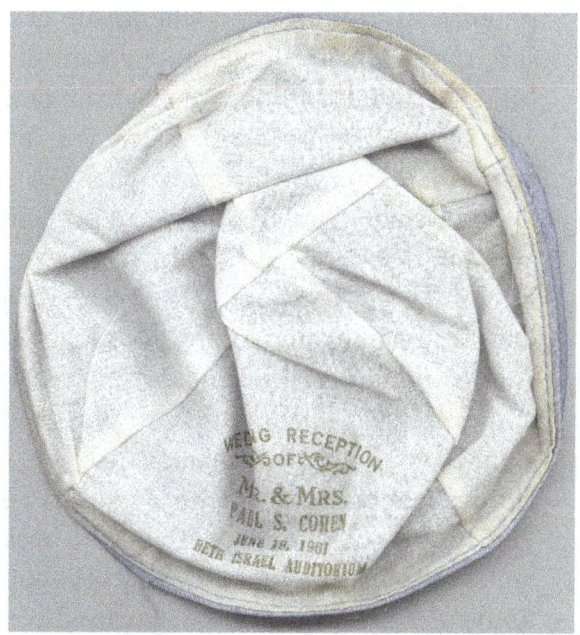

A *yarmulke* with the date and place of a marriage printed inside

- **Skull caps (*kipot* in Hebrew and *yarmulkes* in Yiddish) from weddings or bar and bat mitzvahs:** They may have valuable information such as a name (English and Jewish), a date, and a location stamped inside them. Most people just throw these into a drawer and save them for their interesting colors and patterns, but now you know they have some awesome clues!
- **Birth and marriage certificates:** They provide names, dates, and birthplaces. Don't forget to look for *ketubot* (Jewish marriage contracts).

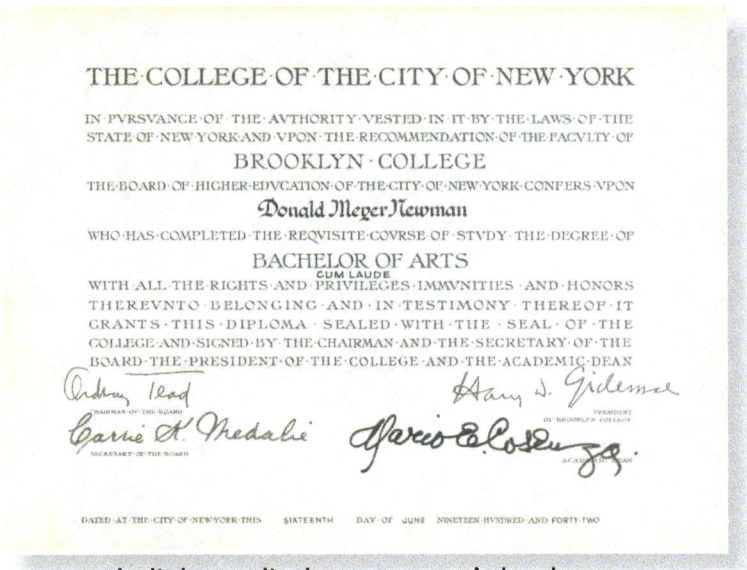

A diploma displays a person's legal name

Front and back of a military medal received by Caryn Alter's spouse's grandfather during World War I

- **Bar and bat mitzvah, *brit milah* (ceremony of circumcision), or baby-naming certificates:** They provide names, dates, and relationships between family members.
- **Photographs:** They can show geographic locations, military uniforms, and local customs. Photos might even have dates and names written on the back.
- **Awards, military service medals, and military documents:** Awards for good scholarship or community service can tell you about that person's life and interests. Military medals and documents from family members who served their country can give you important clues about their lives and historic events.
- **Old newspaper articles:** They can provide details about an event that involved a family member.
- **Diplomas and yearbooks:** They can provide graduation dates and names, and locations of schools.
- **Audio and video recordings:** They can bring to life voices and expressions from everyday events and special occasions of your family members.
- **Naturalization certificates or passports:** They can provide information about relatives who became United States citizens, and interesting facts about their birthplace and their journey to the United States.

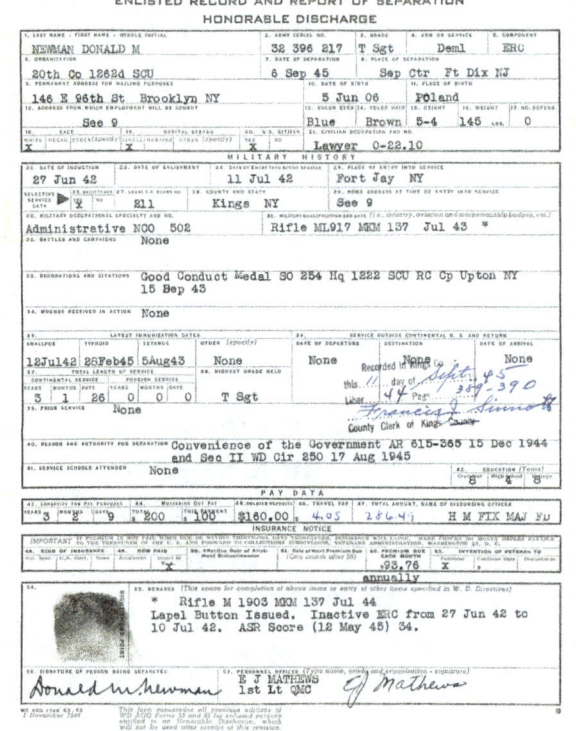

Military discharge document of Stephen Cohen's relative

- **Souvenirs from vacations or visits with relatives:** They can show places and houses and even historical landmarks.
- **Letters and postcards from relatives:** They can give you a glimpse into the lives of your relatives. Some old postcards may even have a photo printed on the front or back.
- **Death certificates and obituaries (death notices in newspapers):** They can provide names, dates, and locations related to the person who died.

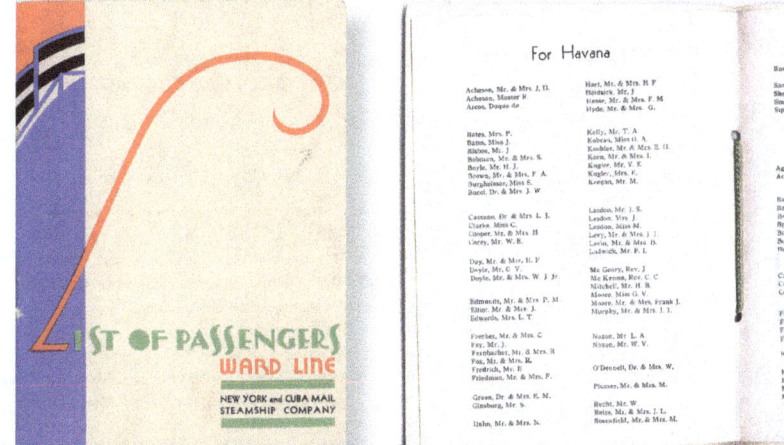

1933 brochure from the honeymoon cruise of Stephen Cohen's relatives

- *Yahrzeit* charts: When a Jew dies, the funeral home often provides a chart with the anniversaries of the date of that person's death (the *yahrzeit*, or "year-time") for the next 20 or so years. This chart would list the date of death.
- **Invitations to weddings, bar or bat mitzvahs, graduations, or other events:** These all list names, dates, and places that are important to a relative's story.
- **Maps of cemeteries where relatives are buried:** They give the locations of graves, and the grave markers provide names (English and Jewish), dates, and other important facts (such as whether the deceased relative was a *Kohen*—more about this in a later chapter!).
- **Traditional Jewish objects like wine cups, Sabbath candlesticks, Hanukkah menorahs, bags to hold a** *tallit*, **and** *siddurim* **(prayer books):** These items may be inscribed with important information and have interesting stories to tell!
- **Real estate documents:** Real estate refers to land or buildings, so documents related to buying and selling land or the buildings on them may have interesting information about your ancestors and where they lived or worked.
- **Inheritance or probate documents:** Inheritance refers to what happens to a person's belongings after that person dies. Do the items get sold or donated to a charity? Are the items given to particular members of the person's family? If a person writes a document called a *will*, the will describes how the person's property is to be distributed to others after that person's death. If the person has no will, then local courts and judges have to decide what to do with the property, a process called *probate*. There may be an old will or probate papers in your house. These papers can contain valuable information about a person's life and family members.
- **Articles in magazines and newspapers, or even entire books:** Perhaps your relative was a journalist or author. Finding that person's own words published for all to see can be exciting for you as a family historian. By reading this relative's article or book, you might learn something about a new topic!

Russian souvenirs that Caryn Alter's cousins brought with them to the United States in the 1970s, when leaving the Soviet Union

12 Genealogy Techniques

A *yahrzeit* chart gives the date of death for a relative

First page of a will written by a relative of Stephen Cohen: Right on the first page it lists the names of the relative's sister and brothers

Which of these types of records from or about your family members can you find in your home? Check off items on this list:

☐ Birth certificates	☐ Real estate documents
☐ Marriage certificates	☐ Diplomas
☐ Death certificates	☐ *Yahrzeit* charts
☐ *Ketubot*	☐ Letters or postcards
☐ *Kipot/yarmulkes* with relatives' events printed inside	☐ Cemetery maps showing where relatives are buried
☐ Bar and bat mitzvah certificates	☐ School yearbooks
☐ Certificates of *brit milah*	☐ Medals and other awards
☐ Photographs	☐ Naturalization certificates
☐ Newspaper articles about relatives	☐ Audio or video recordings
☐ Books or articles written by relatives	☐ Traditional Jewish objects owned or inscribed by relatives
☐ Souvenirs	☐ Wills or other inheritance documents
☐ Invitations	☐ Anything else (list)

Genealogy Techniques 13

Yiddish postcard written by Stephen Cohen's great-grandfather in 1947

Can you read the name of the owner of this old wine cup? (Answer: "*Shlomo Chaim Noyman*")

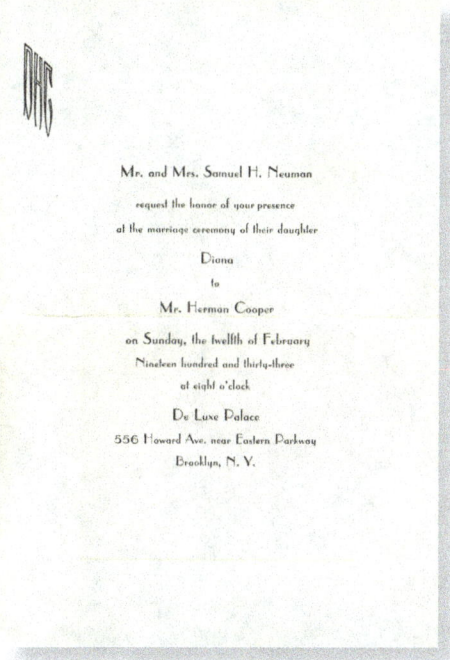

Wedding invitations have the date, place, and names of bride and groom

In this digital age, some family history researchers prefer not to be swamped with paper copies of everything. Instead, they scan the papers and save the images on a computer. This is a perfectly reasonable solution to the "Where do I keep all these things, because my room isn't big enough?" dilemma. Just be sure you name and organize your computer files so you can find them easily, and...**BACK UP YOUR FILES REGULARLY!**

Ask relatives questions! Even though you might sometimes feel like a bit of a pest, your relatives will be proud that you've taken an interest in your family's history.

✡ You Are What You Eat

In addition to hunting in your house for clues like photographs and newspaper clippings, there might be some other less obvious, but still valuable, clues that could be missed.

You know how you've always loved your Grandma Esther's noodle kugel? Or your Uncle Larry's potato latkes? Believe it or not, the way your relatives make their special foods could provide hints regarding your family background.

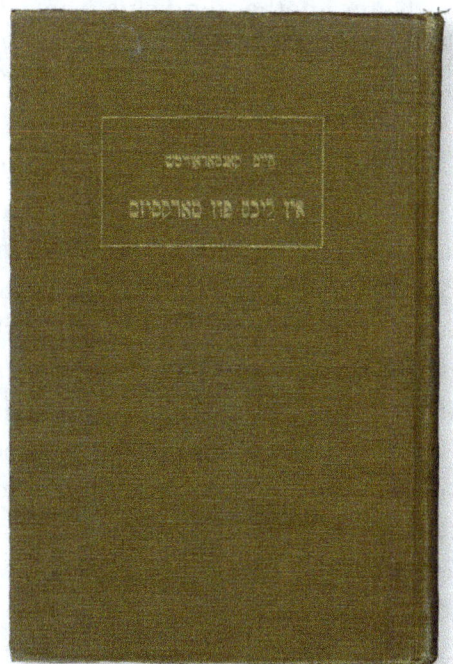

A book in Yiddish, published in 1925, by a relative of Stephen Cohen

For example, if your family serves latkes for Hanukkah with applesauce rather than sour cream, it might be a clue that your ancestors were from southeastern Europe (countries like Romania, Hungary, Ukraine). The Jews from this area of Europe (*Galitsyaner* Jews) favored

14   Genealogy Techniques

Pan de siete cielos (bread of the seven heavens), which Sephardim often bake in honor of the Jewish holiday Shavuot

sweet foods like sweet noodle kugel, applesauce, sweet gefilte fish, and cold sour-cherry soup.

Litvak Jews from northeastern Europe (countries like Estonia, Latvia, Lithuania, Belarus) preferred less sweet foods like plain noodle kugel, sour cream, unsweetened gefilte fish, and shchav (sorrel soup). Jews from the more southern and southwestern areas of Poland tended to prefer sweeter foods, at least partially because sugar refineries that were built there made sugar readily available.

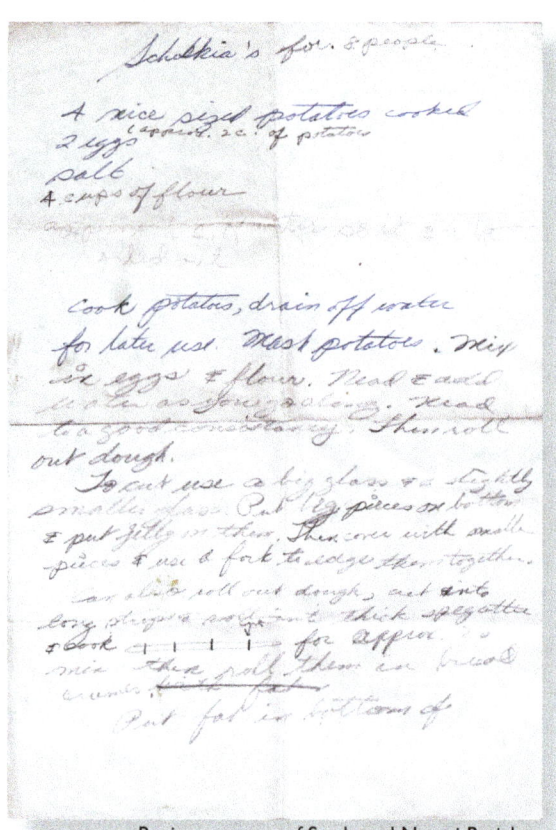

Recipe courtesy of Sandy and Naomi Basickes

Old handwritten recipe for *shlishkes*, a dish local to Hungarian Jews, written by a woman born in Hungary

Here's another food clue: The delicious braided bread eaten at the start of the Sabbath is called *challah* by most Jews, but some Jewish families with origins in Central and Western Europe call it *barkhes* (or *berkhes*)!

Passover can provide clues about ancestral origins: Some Sephardic households give the *beitzah* (roasted egg) to an unmarried family member to eat at the end of the meal. You might wrap the *afikoman* in a sack and put it over your shoulder in a Sephardic home. Ashkenazim often eat *kneydlekh* (matzah balls) at Passover, but they're not as much a Sephardic tradition. Jews from Georgia (not the southern USA state, but the country between Russia and Turkey) add ground walnuts to their *kneydlekh*. Litvaks (Jews of Belarus and Baltic lands) often eat *risel borsht* (fermented beet soup). Syrian Jews often have *kibe* (fried balls made of wheat and meat). North African Jews might have cakes of honey, almond, and cinnamon.

Even the way your family members say certain Jewish words could provide you with some cool clues. To use a food word as an example, some Ashkenazic Jewish families who spoke Yiddish might call a noodle casserole a "*kigl*." Other Ashkenazim may say "*kugl*." Southeastern European (Galitsyaner) Yiddish tends to use the "ih" sound (as in "mitt"), whereas northeastern European Jews (Litvaks) tend to use the "oo" sound (as in "good").

So, if you pay close attention, there might be some terrific genealogy clues right under your nose—or on your dinner plate!

List some special foods that might provide clues to your family's origins.

★ Start Your Engines—Search Engines, That Is!

We truly live in a golden age of genealogy with the Internet as close as the phone in our pocket. Only a short time ago, genealogists had to go to special offices in different cities to view records. Now many of these records have been scanned and placed online.

Some of the online sites are free, and some aren't. Ask a parent if you need to register or pay to gain access to certain databases. Your local public library may even have free access to some of them, so check with the library first.

Artificial intelligence (AI) is the science of developing machines or devices that can think like human beings. AI will play an important role in genealogy research. When combined with traditional genealogy research methods, it might help with analyzing historical documents and save you time when you're searching for facts about your family members. This is an active area of development and we expect improvements to its success rate in the near future.

You will see a lot of information in this book about various online databases that can help you with your family search. Not everything in the world is online, so don't rely only on the Internet. Sometimes there's no substitute for actual printed documents and personal interviews.

★ DNA Testing

Sometimes there just isn't any document to help you, no matter how hard you search. Genealogists call this "hitting a brick wall." What, then, can you do? Here is one possible tool, but **YOU MUST ASK A PARENT IF THEY WOULD CONSIDER DOING THIS OPTION THEMSELVES:**

There are companies that will test a sample of the skin on the inside of a person's mouth to see if it is similar to other people's skin cells. (No, it doesn't hurt. You just swab the inside of your mouth with a tiny wand, put the wand in a small jar, and send the jar in an envelope to the company.)

If you are interested in biology and biochemistry, then this is totally cool stuff to learn about!

The companies test the DNA (short for deoxyribonucleic acid), the molecular instructions that nearly all the cells in your body contain. You inherit DNA from your parents—about 50% from each parent. They inherit about half of their DNA from each of THEIR parents. So you and your cousins have a small portion of DNA in common, and companies can test the DNA to see how closely related you are to other people.

There are several sorts of tests these companies do:

- *Y-DNA.* All males have a Y chromosome; females do not. The Y-DNA is passed directly from father to son. With this test you can directly check your father's ancestry. For example, there is much evidence that male Jews who claim to be descended from *Kohanim* (the High Priests in biblical times) share some of the same Y-DNA.
- *Mitochondrial DNA.* Mitochondria are small parts of every cell in your body, and they contain special DNA that is transmitted from a mother to all her children. You can therefore use mitochondrial DNA tests to discover relationships on your mother's side. This test is better at guessing your general ethnic background, that is, people with whom you share a common cultural background.
- *Autosomal DNA.* This test checks your overall DNA for similarities to others' DNA. The more closely you are related to someone, the more similar the DNA samples would be to each other.

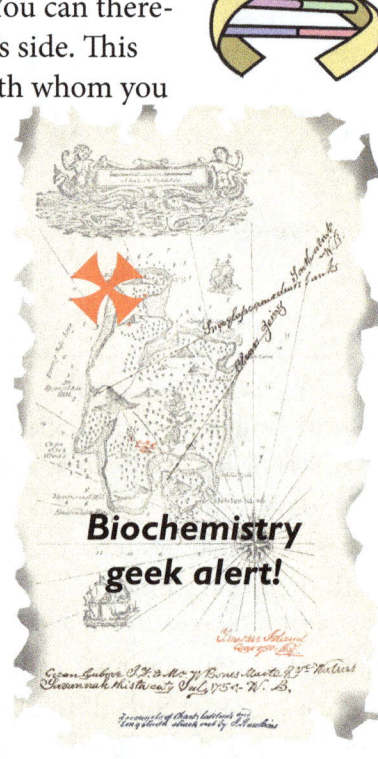

Biochemistry geek alert!

There are advantages and disadvantages to each of these different DNA tests:

- Y-DNA and autosomal DNA tests are able to check for relatively recent relationships (within the last few hundred years, say, five to seven generations).
- Mitochondrial DNA seems to change very slowly over time, so this type of DNA examines the "big picture" over the course of many thousands of years—that is, how population groups migrated across planet Earth. It is less useful for tracking relationships between individuals.

No DNA test can tell you HOW you are related to someone—only IF you are (likely) related, and the closeness of that relationship. You will not get a

REMINDER: DNA tests have minimum age requirements. Therefore, you can ask a parent if they wish to do this kind of test. It costs money, and may involve certain legal issues as well. How to interpret DNA tests is still an ongoing area of genealogical research.

result that says "Joe Levine is your fourth cousin once removed on your mother's side." Rather, you might get a result that says, "Joe Levine may be somewhere between your third and your fifth cousin." You only get a rough guide, not a detailed document, from a DNA test. Yet sometimes it can provide a clue that you would not have found any other way.

DNA-testing companies usually provide you with a list of your ancestral ethnic groups, measured against samples the companies use as a standard. These standard samples are created from people's ancestries that they reported to the DNA-testing company. Therefore, if those people reported incorrect information, those errors are included in the samples the company uses. Also, how the companies define ethnic groups varies.

Sometimes a person's DNA results might show a very small percentage of a particular ethnic group. Scientists call these small percentage errors "noise" in the data. If you decide to study science, you will learn more about these statistical errors, because observations always include some small amount of error.

✡ Recording Your Sources

Making a permanent record of how you obtain information about a relative is an important way to document your findings. This type of record-keeping is also done for all types of scientific and historical research. Bonus: If you plan to be a scientist or historian, learning to keep records will serve you well for your future career!

If you interview a family member, write down the name of the family member, the facts you learned from the person, and the location of the interview. If you find a fact in a published source, write down the source (for example, the title and page number of a book or the name and date of a newspaper). If the fact is in a personal letter or other source that was never published, make a note that the source is unpublished. For example:

Aunt Minnie Schwartz
Born July 4, 1886 in Radomysl, Poland as Malka Shapiro (according to Great-Grandpa Joe Shapiro, who told me this on April 6, 2023)
Emigrated through Ellis Island, New York on June 3, 1906 (from Ellis Island immigration records, on Ancestry.com)
Died September 22, 1956 in Philadelphia, Pennsylvania (according to the obituary in the *Philadelphia Inquirer*, p. 32)
Buried in Degel Yehudo cemetery, Deans, New Jersey (shown on the death certificate)

Sometimes relatives disagree on certain facts. Aunt Anna might say that Great-Grandpa Morris was born in 1906, while Aunt Beckie might say, "No, he was born in 1908." How do you know who is correct? Well, YOU are the detective. Use all the documents you have and—like Sherlock Holmes, the famous fictional detective—arrive at your own conclusions (Holmes had a talent for using just a few important clues to skillfully solve complicated mysteries). Record all your facts and their sources. As you unearth more clues, you may be able to determine which set of facts is more accurate. Part of the fun of genealogy is using your analytical powers and becoming the family history expert.

The Name Game

This book is about finding your ancestors, and that includes their names. For thousands of years, names have held deep meaning in Jewish tradition, so let's explore a bit about Jewish names and traditions about naming.

✡ Ancient Names

To this day, Jews take names from their holy books. Names such as Adam and Chava (or their counterparts in English, Adam and Eve), the first people mentioned in the Bible, are still popular. We find Moshe, Yehoshua, David, Ruth, Tamar, Dina, and many more such ancient names. Names of ancient Jewish royalty, prophets, and heroes, such as David, Shlomo, Miriam, and Naomi continue to be popular as well.

The Book of Esther, interestingly, notes that the heroine of the story, Esther, also had a Hebrew name, Hadassah. This is the first time in history that a Jew was said to have both a Jewish name (Hadassah) and a secular name (Esther). Modern scholarship indicates that the names Esther and Mordechai may have been derived from the names of the Babylonian gods Ishtar and Marduk, although now they are accepted as Jewish names.

King Alexander the Great of the ancient Greek kingdom of Macedon was known for his fair treatment of Jews. As a result, the name Alexander became accepted as a Jewish name as well.

✡ Talmudic Names

During the Roman Empire and early Middle Ages, the Talmud, comprised of stories and legal rulings based on Jewish scripture, was written down. Many of the names of rabbis and figures mentioned in the Talmud, such as Hillel, Beruriah, and Akiva, to name just a few, are still prevalent.

✡ Medieval Names

The medieval period (also called the Middle Ages) was a difficult time for Jews. As the Western Roman Empire collapsed in the 4th and 5th centuries, Jews began naming children for special times or holidays, such as Nisan (the month for Passover), YomTov ("holiday"), or even Shabtai ("the Sabbath"). In those areas where Jews lived under Islamic rule from the 7th century onward, Arabic names occasionally were given to children, including Dunash and Abdala.

By the 9th century, parents sometimes gave two names to boys: a Jewish name to be used when reading the Torah and getting married (*shem hakodesh*, or "holy name"), and a secular name (*kinnui*) for everyday life. Also popular was the tradition of using Jewish names that were repeated every other generation: For example, if you lived during this time, your grandfather might be named David, your father might be named Moshe, and you might be named David.

By the time of the European "High Middle Ages" (11th through 15th century), all sorts of names of non-Jewish origin were being given to Jewish children. This resulted in a decree from rabbis that all Jewish boys needed a "Jewish" name when they were born. Girls, who traditionally didn't get called up to read from the Torah, were not subject to this rule.

Double names for boys might include the secular name Bendit and the Jewish name Baruch, which both mean "blessed." The double names might be somehow associated in meaning, such as the name Volf ("wolf") becoming linked with the name Binyamin (Benjamin in English). This is because Benjamin is referred to as a wolf in the Book of Genesis. Or the names might just sound similar, such as the secular name Anselm and the Biblical name Asher. Later on, rabbis made these associated double names formal.

Common sets of double names, including Dov Ber, Naftali Hirsh, Shlomo Zalman, Yehuda Leyb, Aryeh Leyb, Binyamin Volf, and Rachel Leah, might appear in your own family's history! You may even discover a relative with a secular double name that matches the Jewish double name. Sometimes a person named Dov Ber might be referred to as Dov, sometimes as Ber, and sometimes as both. Be aware that both names may or may not be on your documents.

Many names that Jews adopted during medieval times (which ended about 1450) derive from the regions in which they lived or traveled. So, if the Jews lived for a time in German-speaking kingdoms in Central Europe, they may have adopted names like Falk ("falcon"), Ber ("bear"), Perl ("pearl"), Kreyndl ("little crown"), or Guta ("good"). If they lived at some point in French- or Spanish-speaking areas, perhaps they took names like Beyleh ("pretty"), Estella ("star"), Flora ("flower"), Vital ("life"), or Shprintseh ("hope"). If they lived in Slavic-speaking areas (Polish and Czech languages), maybe they acquired names like Zlata ("gold") or Charna ("black-haired").

Another name Jews used during medieval times was Kalonymus (Greek for "good name").

Double names can be challenging when you research your family.

✡ Nicknames

Nicknames are popular in English, like Bob for Robert and Liz for Elizabeth. Jews have long used nicknames as well. Among some Jewish nicknames invented in medieval times are Kopl (from Ya'akov), Sender (Yiddish for Alexander), Yosl (from Yosef), Shmulik (from Shmuel), Dvoshke (a Russian form of Devora), and even Mariashke (from Maria).

✡ Names and Dialects

Names: The *Ashkenazic* Jews of Europe and Russia had a different way of pronouncing Hebrew than the *Sephardic* Jews, who originated in Spain and Portugal. The letter *tav* with a dot inside (תּ) is pronounced "T" among both Ashkenazim and Sephardim, but the *tav* without a dot (ת) is traditionally pronounced "S" only by the Ashkenazim. The *ayin* (ע) is silent for the Ashkenazim, but many Sephardim pronounce it like an "ng" sound (like the end of the word "song").

The Hebrew accent is also different for the two groups: For Sephardim, the last syllable of a word is usually stressed, but for Ashkenazim, the first syllable is often stressed. This can make even the same name sound different for different Jews. One example is the name we mentioned above, "Shabtai." For Sephardim, it's pronounced "shahb-TIE," but for Ashkenazim, "SHAHB-seh." The name Ruth in English is pronounced "Root" for Sephardim, but "Rooss" for Ashkenazim.

There are some excellent books and online name data bases with reliable and accurate information about both Ashkenazic and Sephardic naming customs.

Dialects: You may have observed that, even though English is spoken throughout the United States and other countries, it can sound quite different depending on where it's spoken. Many people from New York City, for example, call their city "Noo Yawk," and people in Toronto call their city "T'ronno." People in the southeastern part of the United States often have a particular way of saying words that's called a "southern drawl," and those in Yorkshire in northern England also have a distinctive way of speaking. We call these slight variations in speech "dialects."

The Yiddish language also developed many dialects, which had an effect on how Jews in different regions and countries pronounced their names. Most Yiddish speakers (from southeastern or central Europe) pronounce a certain vowel as "oy," but Yiddish speakers using the Litvak (northeastern European) dialect pronounce the same vowel as "ey" (as in "hey!"). Therefore, depending on one's Yiddish dialect, the ancient Hebrew name that's pronounced "Shlomo" by Modern Hebrew-speaking Israelis and Sephardim can be pronounced "SHLOY-meh" by non-Litvaks or "SHLEY-meh" by Litvaks. In southeastern Europe, a form of the Biblical name Moshe might be "Moysheh," but in northeastern Europe, it might be "Meysheh."

Stephen Cohen's baby book confirms his Litvak origins:
His great-grandfather's Hebrew name, "Shlomo," was pronounced "Shleymeh"

One distinction among Yiddish dialects is that the Litvak dialect uses the vowel "oo," but the others tend to use "ee" for the same syllable. For example, the Yiddish word for "aunt" might be *moomeh* (Litvak dialect) or *meemeh* (other dialects) depending on your family's heritage.

Another dialect difference is the vowel sound that is pronounced as "aw" by Litvaks, but pronounced as "oo" by other Yiddish speakers. For example, the Hebrew name Baruch is "BAW-rekh" among Litvaks, and "BOO-rekh" among other Yiddish speakers. Likewise, the Hebrew name Sarah is "SAW-reh" among Litvaks, and "SOO-reh" among other Yiddish speakers.

It's important for modern Jewish genealogists to be aware of these dialect differences. If your family came from the Russian Empire, you may find names like the ones mentioned above written out in Russian letters in old records. Now you'll know how to pronounce them as they were spoken by your ancestors many years ago!

✡ Jews' Clues

The clues we are talking about here are last names (surnames). The study of Jewish surnames could fill many books (and has!). For nearly all of Jewish history, Jews were referred to by something called a *patronymic* (a name derived from the name of their father).

Here are some examples: In the Torah, Moses's successor was called Joshua ben Nun (Joshua son of Nun). Rabbi Elazar ben Azarya (Elazar son of Azarya) from the Talmud is mentioned in the Passover Haggadah. And there was a famous medieval Sephardic rabbi named Moshe ben Maimon (Moshe son of Maimon) who was more commonly known as Maimonides. Cool fact: "-ides" is Greek for "son of."

Having a last name or family name is a relatively recent development for Jews. In medieval times, some Sephardim acquired last names, and a small handful of Ashkenazim also took last names, especially when Jewish communities in cities became too large to be able to differentiate between multiple "David ben Shmuels." In the late 1700s and early 1800s, many European countries required all people, including Jews, to take a last name.

This becomes tricky for family researchers like us: Records of our ancestors prior to the early 1800s probably don't list any last names—because they didn't have last names! "Hitting a brick wall," as some researchers would call this challenge, can seem discouraging at first. But by using your detective skills, and focusing on your ancestor's homeland and family members' names that you know, you might be able to trace your family back to the 1700s or earlier!

Precisely why people adopted specific last names is a story often lost to history. Let's just say that your surname may be a clue to your background as well.

Ashkenazic Naming Customs: If your ancestors were *Kohanim* ("ancient High Priests"), your surname may be Cohen, Kogan (the Russian language has no "h," so a "g" is used instead), Kahane, Kaplan (in Polish *kapłan* means "priest"), or Katz. Why Katz? It has nothing to do with cats, but is because Katz is written in Hebrew as כ״ץ, which is an acronym (an abbreviation that you pronounce) for *Kohen Tzedek* ("righteous priest"). If your ancestors were *Levi'im* ("assistants to the high priests"), your surname may be Levi, Levin, Levine, or Segal. Why Segal? Because Segal is probably an acronym for *Segan leKohen*, "assistant to the High Priest."

The suffix "-witz" (or "-wicz" or "-vitch") is Slavic for "son of," so you might be able to guess that somebody named Josefovitch had an ancestor named Josef or Yosef. Likewise, the Slavic suffix "-kin" means "child of the mother named," so somebody named Nechamkin could be the descendant of a woman named Nechama. Polish, Russian, and Ukrainian are examples of Slavic languages.

But many people with the surname Horowitz or Gurewicz (again a Russian "g" instead of "h") are not descended from a man named "Hor." Instead, this name comes from a Czech town, Hořovice. People with this surname are possibly descended from Rabbi Yeshayahu HaLevi *Ish-Horowitz* (Hebrew for "man from Hořovice"), who moved to Prague in the early 1600s. Rabbi Yeshayahu was a *Levi*, so many Jewish genealogists think that people who are *Levi'im* with the name Horowitz are related.

Sephardic Naming Customs: Among Sephardim, many Jews have surnames derived from Hebrew, Spanish, Portuguese, or Arabic. Cohen and Levi are common, of course, but so are Abravanel, Cardoza, Gabbay ("tax collector"), Hazan ("cantor"), Rabi ("rabbi"), Montefiore (Monte = Italian for "mountain" and fiore = Italian for "flower"), Serfati ("Frenchman," from the Hebrew *Tsarfat* for "France"), and so on. Search some Jewish or Sephardic genealogy websites for detailed information about Sephardic surnames.

Mizrahi Naming Customs: *Mizrahi* Jews (with origins in the Middle East and North Africa) also have surnames based on professions (Hakim = "doctor," Kafashian = "shoe-dealer"), Hebrew words (Baroukh = "blessed," Hai = "living"), or geography (Esfahani, Shomroni, Tehrani).

Of course, all bets are off if your family's surname was changed after emigration to a new land. For example, one of the authors has the surname Cohen, but his ancestors were not *Kohanim*—the surname was changed after arrival in America.

Many Eastern European Jewish surnames are derived from the Yiddish or German languages. Jewish surnames may be related to:

- **Places:** Shapiro (from the town of Speyer, pronounced "SHPY-er," in Germany), Posner (from the Polish city of Posen), Vilner or Wilner (from the Yiddish name Vilna, referring to the city of Vilnius in Lithuania), Pollack (literally "a person from Poland")
- **Jobs or occupations:** Ackerman ("plowman"), Blecher ("tinsmith," for *blekh* is Yiddish for "sheet tin"), Shuster ("shoemaker"), Schneider ("tailor"), Apteker ("pharmacist"), Bronfman ("whisky distiller")
- **Religious titles:** Rabin ("rabbi"), Kantor ("cantor")
- **Personal characteristics:** Lang ("long/tall"), Kurz ("short"), Ehrlich ("honest"), Kluger/Kliger ("wise/clever")
- **Animals:** Adler ("eagle"), Loeb ("lion"), Helfand or Gelfand ("elephant"), Taub ("dove"), or Fink ("finch")

- **Plants:** Nusblatt ("nut leaf"), Applebaum ("apple tree"), Rosen ("roses")
- **Foods:** Kirsh ("cherry"), Kigel ("pudding/casserole"), Zucker ("sugar")

Sometimes the names aren't derived from German or Yiddish, but instead from Russian or other Slavic languages. For instance, the surname Kravitz comes from the Ukrainian word for "tailor," and the surname Portnoy comes from the Russian word for "tailor."

Some family names are derived from Hebrew or Aramaic. The names Sofer ("scribe"), Malamud/Melamed ("teacher"), Shoykhet ("kosher slaughterer"), Maggid ("travelling preacher"), and Margolis ("pearl") are commonly found among Jews.

Be aware that having a friend with the same last name as you doesn't automatically mean that the two of you are cousins. Often people in different parts of Europe chose, or were given, the same surname. You have to research the two families to find a common ancestor before you can say you and your friend are really related.

When researching your ancestors, it will be more effective to concentrate on the first names of people in your family rather than the surname. Our ancestors often changed surnames depending on time, place, and political circumstances, so focusing on just a family name or last name may be a less valuable use of your time. And, as mentioned, most Jews didn't even have family names until fairly recently in Jewish history anyway.

✡ Baby-Naming Customs

It's important to remember that Ashkenazic Jews from Eastern and Central Europe had different customs for naming their children than Sephardic Jews, descendants of the Jews who lived on the Iberian Peninsula (Spain, Portugal, Andorra, and Gibraltar) from before the first century until their expulsion in 1492.

Ashkenazic Jews generally name their children after relatives who are no longer living. Often parents name a child for a relative who has not yet been honored by having a baby named for him or her. Another tradition is to name the baby for its mother if the mother died in childbirth, or for its father, if the father died while the mother was pregnant (fortunately, both are rare occurrences now).

Sephardic Jews may name their children after living relatives. For example, Sephardic Jews usually name the first-born son after his father's father (paternal grandfather); the second son is named after his mother's father (maternal grandfather). Likewise, the first-born daughter is named after her father's mother (paternal grandmother); the second daughter is named after her mother's mother (maternal grandmother).

Knowing Jewish naming customs will be helpful when you search for names of your relatives. Are you Ashkenazic, Sephardic, Mizrahi, Italian, Yemenite, Greek, Beta Israel (Ethiopian), something else, or a mixture of Jewish groups?

Your Family's Names

List any naming customs in your family	
List surnames (last names) that were common among your ancestors	
Give the meanings of these surnames	

You and Your Family

Now that you know some basic techniques for finding your ancestors, it's time to get to work. Your first task is to record information about you and your family to start your family tree.

✡ Write What You Know

You may be surprised to discover that you're more of a genealogy sleuth than you realize. For instance, you may already know some of these important facts about your family members:

- Their English and Jewish names, and possibly nicknames
- The year they were born
- Their birthplace
- Where they lived as children and as adults
- What they did for their job

Using these facts as clues can help you unearth additional genealogy gems about people in your family tree.

Let's start with YOU.

Your birth date	
Your birthplace (including the exact town)	
Your Jewish name (if you have one)	
The special reason for this name (if there is one)	
Places where you have lived	
Historical events the year you were born	
Your interests and hobbies	

You and Your Family

If you have a sibling (sister or brother), fill in the chart below. If you have more than one sibling, copy the chart as many times as you need and staple the chart(s) to this page.

Sibling's name	
Sibling's birthday	
Sibling's birthplace (including the exact town)	
Sibling's Jewish name (if sibling has one)	
The special reason for this name (if there is one)	
Historical events the year sibling was born	
Sibling's interests and hobbies (other than being annoying!)	

Now do the same for your parent or parents:

Parent's name	
Parent's birthday	
Parent's birthplace (including the exact town)	
Parent's Jewish name (if the parent has one)	
The special reason for this name (if there is one)	
Places parent has lived other than birthplace	
Parent's occupation and interests	

Another parent's name

Parent's name	
Parent's birthday	
Parent's birthplace (including the exact town)	
Parent's Jewish name (if the parent has one)	
The special reason for this name (if there is one)	
Places parent has lived other than birthplace	
Parent's occupation and interests	

As you go further back in time, these charts can get more interesting.

Here is a chart for one grandparent. Copy it for any other grandparents, and fill in the charts as best as you can. Ask a parent for help. Staple the extra chart(s) to this page.

One grandparent's name	
Grandparent's birthday	
Grandparent's birthplace (including the exact town)	
Grandparent's Jewish name (if the grandparent has one)	
The special reason for this name (if there is one)	
Places grandparent has lived other than birthplace	
Grandparent's occupation and interests	
If your grandparent is no longer living, list the date and place (town/country) of the death	
If your grandparent is no longer living, write down the name of their cemetery and the town where it is located	

You and Your Family

Your family members may not know all the answers to these questions. That's okay. But with some clues for starters, you can put on your detective hat and find them out on your own.

✱ Genealogy and Math

If you are a math whiz, then have we got some genealogical fun for you!

Just like a maple tree can have lots of different branches from top to bottom, a family tree can show you all the "branches" or relationships between people in your family. Even though you might not personally know every single relative in your family tree, here is how the branches will start growing:

- Two parents (one generation back)
- Four grandparents (two generations back)
- Eight great-grandparents (three generations back)

Let's do a little math to show you how quickly your family tree will blossom.

First, let's make a table using the example of two parents:

Ancestor	Generations Back	Number of Ancestors in Each Generation
You (We realize you aren't your own ancestor)	0	1
Parents	1	2
Grandparents	2	4
Great-grandparents	3	8
Great-great-grandparents	4	16
Skip a bunch of "greats"	...	...
Great × 10 grandparents	12	4096

Here is an equation to calculate the number of ancestors for each generation:

Number of ancestors = $2^{\text{(generations back)}}$

If you haven't learned the "exponentiation" or "power" idea in math, let's write it out for six generations back:

Number of ancestors = $2 \times 2 \times 2 \times 2 \times 2 \times 2 = 64$

That is, we multiply two by itself six times (the number of generations back), to get 64 ancestors.

Let's take a guess that each generation spans about 25 years (25 is an estimated age at which parents might have children). This is what scientists call a "back-of-the-envelope" calculation, designed to give a rough idea of the size of the answer we are seeking. Then how far back is 12 generations, the last line of the table?

12 generations × 25 years per generation = 300 years (and 4096 ancestors)

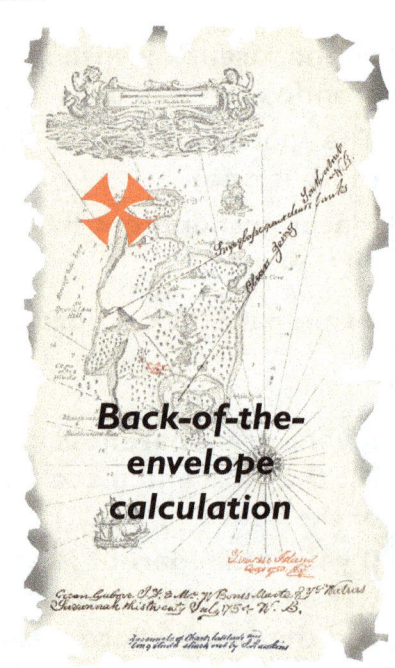

Back-of-the-envelope calculation

Now let's approach this from another direction. Did you ever wonder how many ancestors you might have had at the time the Second Temple in Jerusalem was destroyed in 70 CE, about 1950 years ago?

$$\frac{1950 \text{ years}}{25 \text{ years per generation}} = 78 \text{ generations back}$$

How many ancestors did you have 78 generations ago?

Number of ancestors = $2^{78} = 3 \times 10^{23}$ ancestors!

That's 3 followed by 23 zeros, or 300 sextillion (that's a real number!)

How do we explain this gigantic number of ancestors? Because all people in the world are related to one another, even if only distantly. Everybody has to have some ancestors in common with everyone else. The technical term that genealogists use for this is *pedigree collapse*. Every person's pedigree (or complete ancestry tree) simply cannot be as large as we calculated above. Sometimes people married their relatives (sounds weird, but it's true!), so some of your ancestors have to be counted multiple times.

In many areas, cousins may have married each other (although this is less common nowadays). The cousins' families probably knew each others' backgrounds, making it more likely that a *shidekh* (Yiddish for "match") and then a wedding would occur.

✡ Ask Your Relatives to Add More

You may have noticed that most people love talking about their lives and their pasts. Everyone appreciates an audience! Being a good listener is one of the most important tools of a history detective.

After you've gathered some basic facts like the ones listed earlier, try to fill in the gaps with interesting stories from your family members. It's like starting to write a book report with just a basic outline, and then expanding on that outline to bring the story to life.

Personal stories and tales from the past are precious snippets of history that can never be found in record books or passports. For instance, you might know your grandfather's Jewish name. But perhaps you can ask your grandfather if he is named after a relative. If the answer is yes, maybe he has heard special stories about that relative. You may find out that he was named after a favorite uncle, and you may even discover that other relatives were named after the same uncle.

After doing this a few times, with charts for each relative, you may decide that a looseleaf binder would be a handy way to store all your new information. You may even decide to use genealogy computer software to start saving and organizing all the information you collect: This is what we, the authors, do! For advice as to which computer program is best for you, contact a local genealogy club. They will be overjoyed that a young person like you is interested in a lifelong hobby, and will be glad to help.

This portrait of one of Stephen Cohen's great-grandmothers was painted after her death in 1925 from a photograph taken at a funeral she attended. This is why she has a sad expression. Only by interviewing relatives did the author discover why she looks this way.

✡ Visit and Do a Mitzvah

The biggest mitzvah of all is to visit your family members and speak with them in person about your family history project. Grandparents, aunts, uncles, cousins—they almost always appreciate visits from people who are interested in their life stories. We realize that it's fun and easy to text people, but there is truly nothing like meeting a new (or favorite) relative in person.

Don't forget to record the information that you gather during these visits. You may be quite sure that you'll remember everything that was said, but precious facts may eventually be forgotten if they're not written down or recorded in some way.

Later on in this book, we will show you how to preserve for the future all this information that you have so carefully collected!

Contact a local genealogy club!

 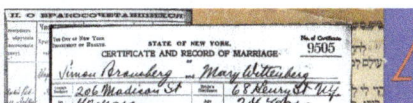  

Watch Your Words

As you begin your genealogy quest, no doubt you may find some papers, books, or photographs with unusual languages on them. Part of the fun of Jewish genealogy is learning to recognize some of these languages, almost like deciphering secret codes. In this chapter, we talk about some important Jewish languages and specific alphabets and scripts, all of which will be valuable when you research your ancestors.

★ Hebrew

Hebrew is the most ancient language—with the oldest writings—of the Jewish people. The Torah, also known as the Five Books of Moses, is thousands of years old.

The Hebrew language is classified as a Semitic language, a family that also includes Arabic. Hebrew is written from right to left, and technically only the consonants are written. Language lovers can impress their friends with the fact that an alphabet consisting only of consonants is called an *abjad*. Adding the vowels as dots and lines above, below, and inside letters came about in the early Middle Ages (late 5th century to the 10th century), when Hebrew had become solely a written language, to help preserve the pronunciation.

Hebrew is the only language in the world successfully revived as a spoken language, which occurred in Palestine in the late 19th century. Prior to that time, Hebrew was a sacred language used only for religious purposes. Linguists (people who study the structure and function of languages) also classify Hebrew as a Jewish language, because it is used primarily by Jews and written with the Hebrew alphabet.

Where do you find Hebrew? In sacred books and scrolls such as a Torah, in prayer books, in the Passover Haggadah, on gravestones, and often in Jewish community record books. Therefore, junior Jewish genealogy detectives will find it useful to learn the Hebrew alphabet, which will help them in their research to recognize certain Jewish names and important genealogy words like "born," "married," "died," "son," "daughter," and "wife."

Many documents, including letters and *ketubot* (Jewish marriage contracts), were written in Hebrew handwriting. The Hebrew script you will learn if you study modern Hebrew was invented in the late Middle Ages, but some Hebrew characters may look different in old documents. Learning Hebrew script is a valuable tool to unlock your family's history.

Example of Hebrew: This is a page from an old printing of the Book of Esther; the dots and lines in and near the letters serve as vowels and as a form of musical notation so you know how to chant the story

✡ Aramaic

Aramaic is another Jewish language, for it was used by Jews and written with the Hebrew alphabet. Like Hebrew, it uses an abjad, with only consonants written. There are several dialects of Aramaic, including Syriac, which is spoken by some Christians in the Middle East. In this book, we will focus only on Jewish Aramaic.

Aramaic, like Hebrew, is also an ancient language and dates from nearly 3000 years ago. You will find Aramaic in prayer books, in a few sections of the Jewish Bible, in a *ketubah*, and in the song "*Chad Gadya*" in the Passover Haggadah. It is much less likely to be useful when tracing your family history because, although the bulk of the *ketubah* is written in Aramaic, the names and places mentioned in a marriage contract are more likely to be spelled in Hebrew.

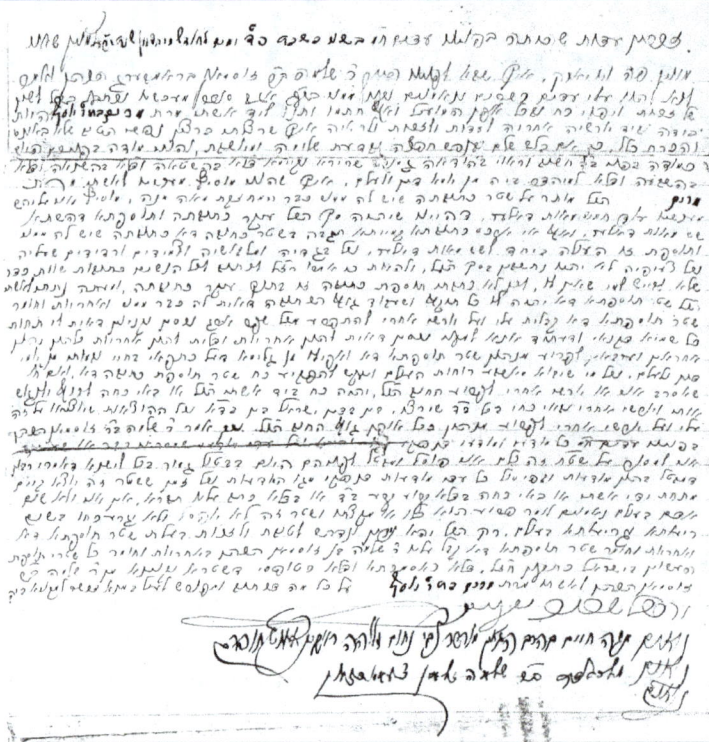

Addition to a handwritten Aramaic ketubah of one of Stephen Cohen's relatives, 1909

✡ Yiddish

Yiddish is the common language of the Ashkenazim (Jews originating in Central and Eastern Europe) from medieval times onward. The earliest records of Yiddish date back nearly 1000 years. It is a language closely related to modern German, so it is classified as a Germanic language—as are English, Swedish, and Dutch. There are many words borrowed from Hebrew, Aramaic, Slavic, and even Old French. But Yiddish is also a Jewish language, spoken almost entirely by Jews and written with the Hebrew alphabet.

Interestingly, by the time Yiddish developed, Jews had started using certain Hebrew letters as vowels, so—unlike with Hebrew—you will find very few dots and lines around the Yiddish letters. Around the year 1900, about 90% of all Jews around the world spoke Yiddish. Following the Holocaust and, later on, the assimilation of Jews into the cultures of various countries, far fewer Jews now speak Yiddish. But you can find organizations like *Yugntruf*—Youth for Yiddish that will be happy to help you learn the language.

When studying your family history, you are likely to encounter Yiddish written in personal letters and cards, some newspaper articles, and Yizkor Books (memorial books written to commemorate Jewish communities that were destroyed during the Holocaust). We'll discuss Yizkor Books more in a later chapter.

Example of Yiddish: This book on geology by Dr. Abraham Caspe was published in 1918

✡ Ladino

This is the common language of the Sephardim (Jews originating from the Iberian peninsula, now Spain and Portugal) from early medieval times. It is known among Sephardim by different names such as Judeo-Espagnol, Dzhudezmo, Espanyol, or Haketia. It is a language closely related to Spanish, so linguists classify it as a Romance language, like Spanish, French, and Italian.

Like Yiddish, Ladino includes many words of Hebrew and Aramaic origin. Dialects of Ladino in the Ottoman Empire also included some Turkish words. Ladino, like Hebrew and Yiddish, is also considered a Jewish language—it is spoken by Jews, and usually written in the Hebrew alphabet. Also, like Yiddish, Ladino uses some Hebrew letters as vowels, but in a different way than Yiddish. As a result, someone who can read Yiddish would have a very difficult time sounding out the Ladino words, and vice versa. Often Ladino books are printed using the Hebrew typeface called Rashi script, which developed in the 15th century from Sephardic styles of handwriting, as you can see in the example to the right. The American Ladino League may be able to help you learn Ladino.

Family history information in Ladino may be found in newspapers, books, and personal letters. Such letters might be written in Solitreo script, a special cursive form of Hebrew writing. There are some Sephardic synagogues that have prayers in Ladino, and occasionally you can find Ladino songs such as "*Ken Supiese*" in the Passover Haggadah.

A page from a translation of Daniel Defoe's book *Robinson Crusoe* into Ladino, printed in 1896–1897 using Rashi script (Collection in the New York Public Library)

✡ Russian

Russian is not a Jewish language, but if your family originated in the old Russian Empire, you will likely have to learn the Russian alphabet in order to understand documents about your relatives.

Russian is a Slavic language like Polish, Bulgarian, and Ukrainian. Most, but not all, Slavic languages are written in the Cyrillic alphabet, invented in the 890s by students of Saint Cyril, who was from Greece. Many of its letters are based on the Greek alphabet, but the "sh" sound doesn't exist in Greek, so the inventors borrowed the Hebrew letter *shin* (ש) for the letter Ш (called *sha*). English-speakers are often confused by the Cyrillic alphabet letters because some look like the Roman alphabet—but aren't pronounced the same.

Town minutes from the town of Lakhva (now in Belarus) from 1885: Here is printed Russian, including some letters of the alphabet that the Soviet Union later stopped using, and handwritten Russian

The Russian government printed many of its civil records in Russian, and the officials who filled in the documents wrote in Russian handwriting. Like your friends and teachers, sometimes their handwriting was good—and sometimes it was sloppy. After the Russian Revolution overthrew the old Russian Empire in the early 1900s, the Soviet government decided to remove some letters it thought were unnecessary from the Russian alphabet. Because many Jewish records date from the Russian Empire, you will want to learn to read the older style of Russian alphabet letters.

✡ *Fraktur*

Fraktur is not a language, but a type of script. It was used in old German printing, and was phased out by the Nazis during World War II. This style of script might also be called Gothic Script. The name "Fraktur" comes from the Latin word *fractura*, meaning "a break," because the letters look broken up. Calligraphers, those who write text artistically, call it "blackletter."

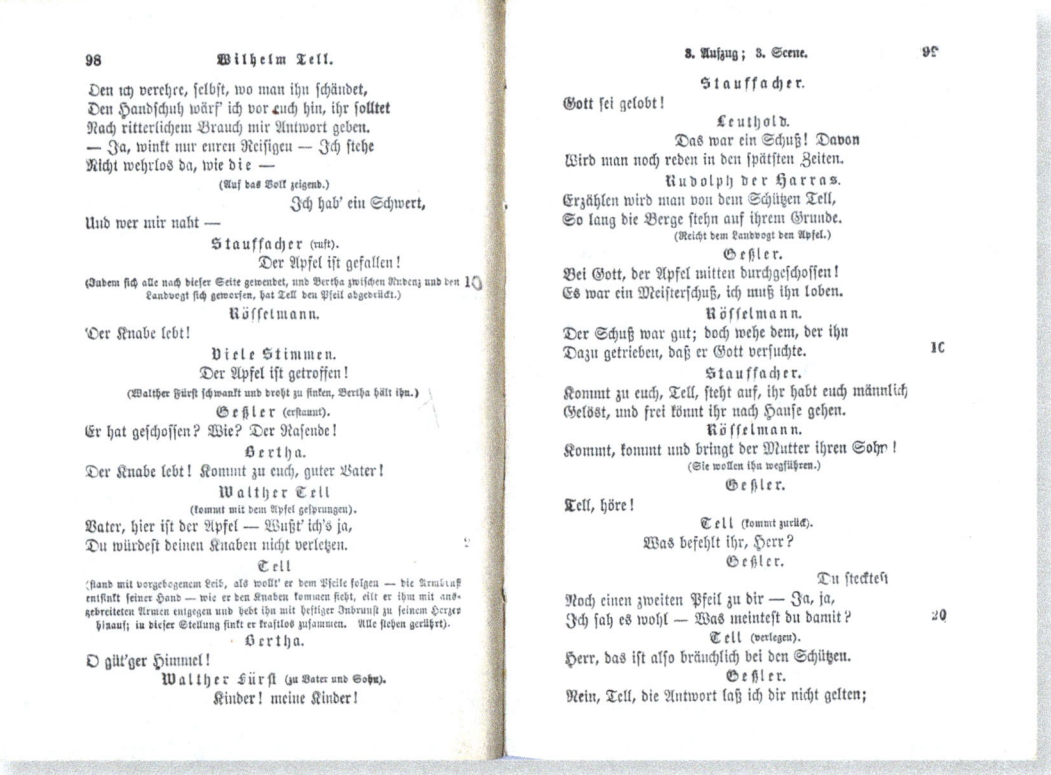

Two pages printed in Fraktur typeface from the German play *Wilhelm Tell*, by Friederich von Schiller, 1877: You may know the story as "William Tell"

Though Fraktur developed from the "blackletter" or Gothic-style handwriting of the Middle Ages, the first documents printed in Fraktur were made in the early 1500s. Nearly all German documents were printed using the Fraktur style through the early 20th century. Therefore, if your family comes from Germany, you may have to learn to read this type of script.

✡ **Kurrent** *and* **Sütterlin**

Kurrent also is not a language, but rather another handwriting style popular in Germany, dating back to the Middle Ages. If your German family documents were printed in Fraktur, the official handwriting on those documents might have been in the *Kurrent* handwriting style.

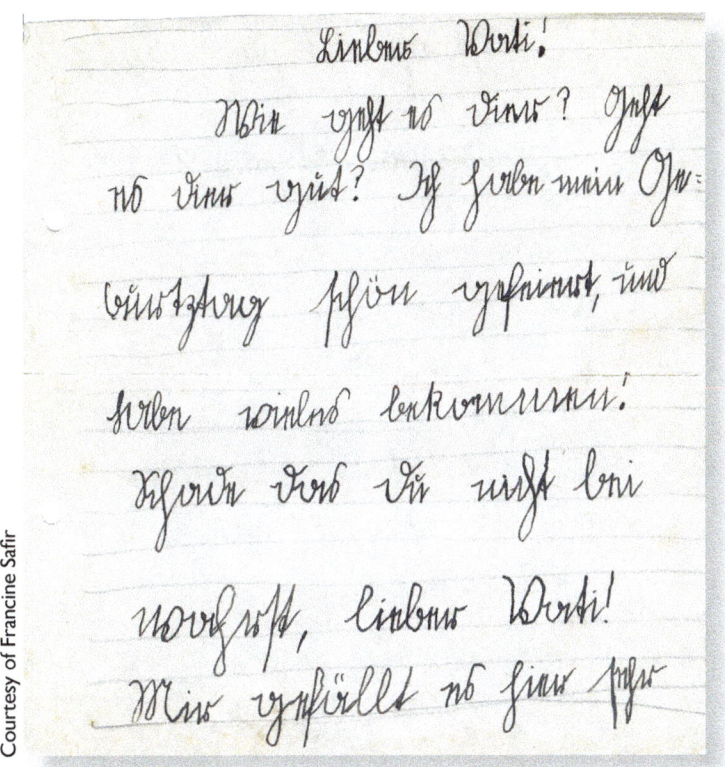 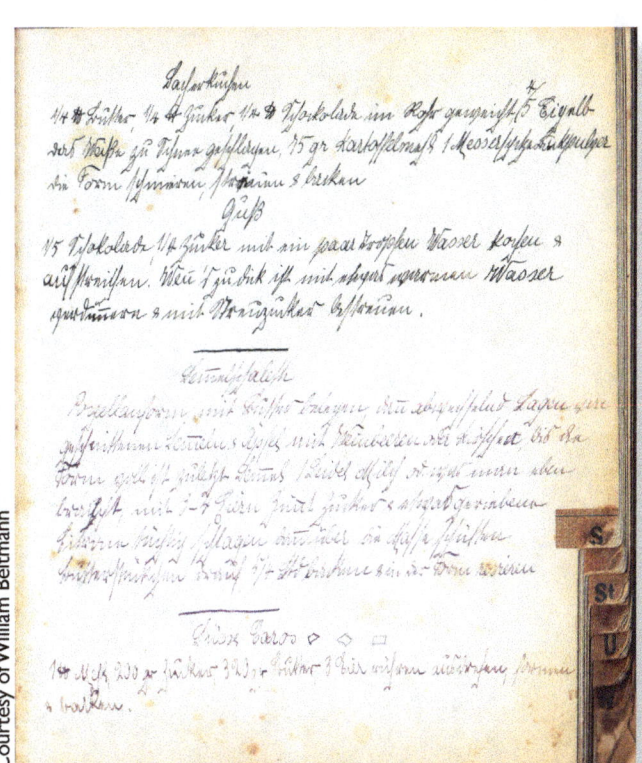

Example of *Sütterlin* handwriting in a child's letter to his father

Example of *Kurrent* handwriting from a homemade German recipe book

In the early 20th century, the *Kurrent* style was simplified into a modern handwriting script called *Sütterlin*, which is perhaps even more difficult to read! Like Fraktur, *Sütterlin* was banned by the Nazis in Germany. If you want to be able to decipher older German documents, you'll have to learn the shapes of the letters in the *Kurrent* or *Sütterlin* handwriting styles.

Artificial intelligence (AI) tools for converting handwriting to printed text may prove helpful in deciphering family documents that are difficult to read. We anticipate that their accuracy will improve in the coming years.

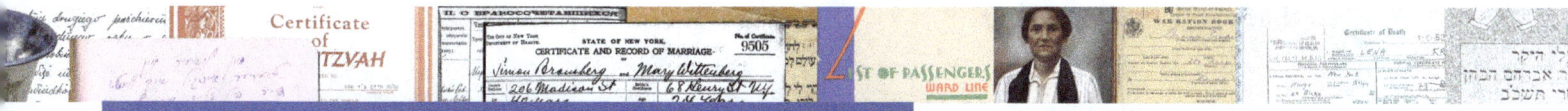

Go Back in Time

NOW THAT YOU KNOW about your immediate family, let's take a trip back in time, using records about your family that you can find online and elsewhere.

★ Census Records

One, two, three, four…learning to count is probably one of your earliest memories. As a small child, you likely learned the importance of counting things correctly, whether they were your fingers or your toys.

Counting is important in genealogy as well, and census records are a valuable resource. Taking a *census* involves counting the number of people in a country, city, or town, and recording information about those people.

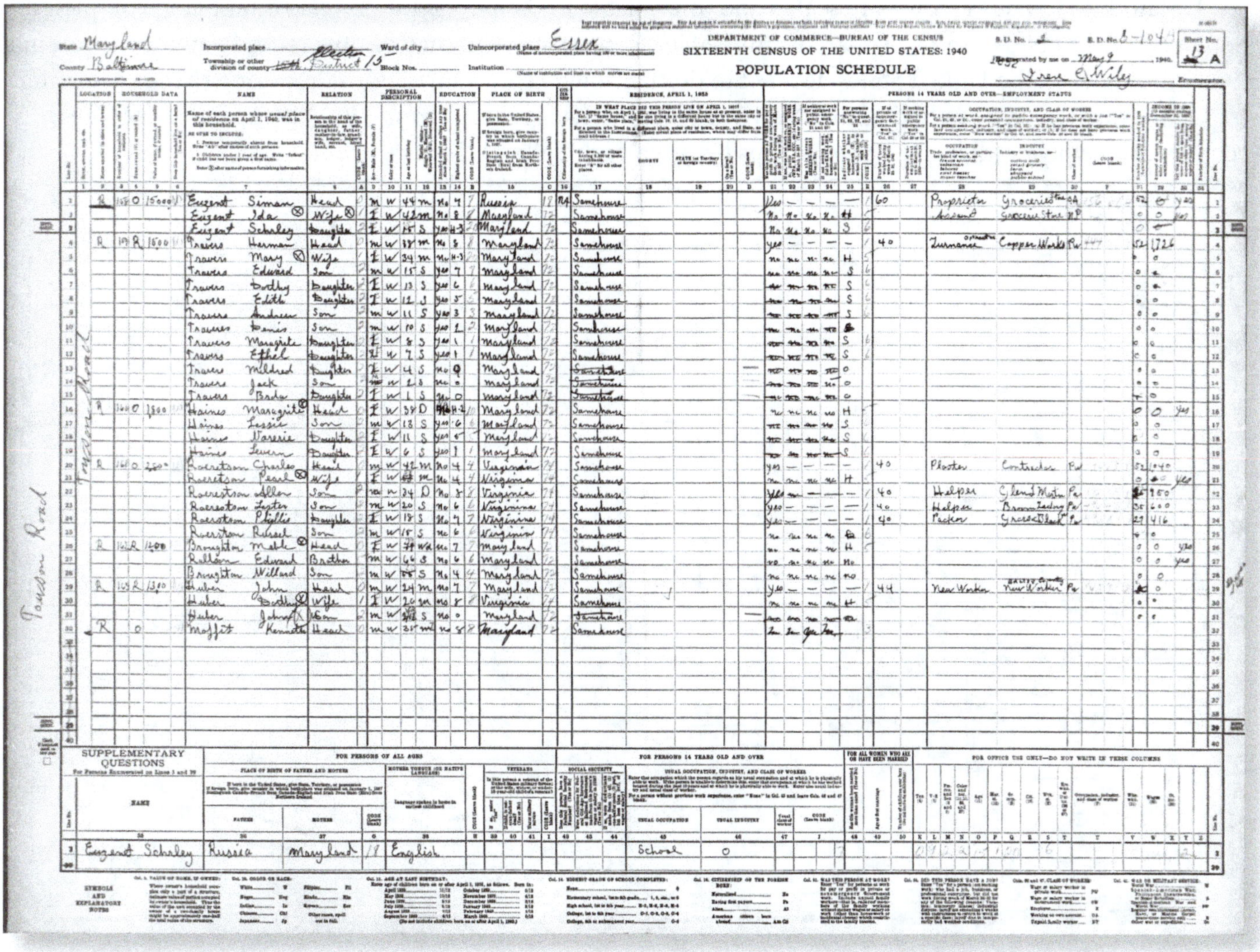
DEPARTMENT OF COMMERCE—BUREAU OF THE CENSUS
SIXTEENTH CENSUS OF THE UNITED STATES: 1940
POPULATION SCHEDULE

State: Maryland. County: Baltimore. Unincorporated place: Essex. Township or other division of county: 15th Election District. Sheet No. 13 A. Enumerated by me on May 9, 1940.

Line	Name	Relation	Sex	Race	Age	Marital status	Place of birth
1	Euzent, Siman	Head	M	W	44	M	Russia
2	Euzent, Ida	Wife	F	W	42	M	Maryland
3	Euzent, Schaley	Daughter	F	W	15	S	Maryland
4	Travers, Herman	Head	M	W	37	M	Maryland
5	Travers, Mary	Wife	F	W	34	M	Maryland
6	Travers, Edward	Son	M	W	15	S	Maryland
7	Travers, Dorothy	Daughter	F	W	13	S	Maryland
8	Travers, Edith	Daughter	F	W	12	S	Maryland
9	Travers, Andrew	Son	M	W	11	S	Maryland
10	Travers, Dennis	Son	M	W	10	S	Maryland
11	Travers, Margaret	Daughter	F	W	8	S	Maryland
12	Travers, Ethel	Daughter	F	W	7	S	Maryland
13	Travers, Mildred	Daughter	F	W	4	S	Maryland
14	Travers, Jack	Son	M	W	2	S	Maryland
15	Travers, Bride	Daughter	F	W	1	S	Maryland
16	Haines, Marguerite	Head	F	W	38	D	Maryland
17	Haines, Lessie	Son	M	W	13	S	Maryland
18	Haines, Marcie	Daughter	F	W	11	S	Maryland
19	Haines, Lewen	Daughter	F	W	6	S	Maryland
20	Roerstson, Charles	Head	M	W	42	M	Virginia
21	Roerstson, Pearl	Wife	F	W	42	M	Virginia
22	Roerstson, Allen	Son	M	W	24	D	Virginia
23	Roerstson, Lester	Son	M	W	20	S	Virginia
24	Roerstson, Phyllis	Daughter	F	W	18	S	Virginia
25	Roerstson, Russell	Son	M	W	15	S	Virginia
26	Broughton, Mabel	Head	F	W	44	Wd	Maryland
27	Rollon, Edward	Brother	M	W	46	S	Maryland
28	Broughton, Willard	Son	M	W	15	S	Maryland
29	Huber, John	Head	M	W	24	M	Maryland
30	Huber, Dorothy	Wife	F	W	20	M	Virginia
31	Huber, John	Son	M	W	0	S	Maryland
32	Moffit, Kenneth	Head	M	W	35	M	Maryland

SUPPLEMENTARY QUESTIONS: Euzent, Schaley — Russia — Maryland — English — School

A page of the United States Federal Census, taken in 1940: This page lists the people living on part of a single street in Baltimore, Maryland

Census records can give you information about your relatives that can include:

- Location of their home

- Names of other household residents (people living in the home of your relatives)
- Jobs or occupations of all the household residents

Even in the Torah portion ("*parasha*") called *Parashat B'midbar* ("In the Desert"), which is in the Book of Numbers, counting is the main theme. *Parashat B'midbar* opens with the taking of a census to determine the number of men over the age of 20 in each of the 12 Israelite Tribes who could form an army to cross the desert.

Fast-forward to the year 1790, the first year that a census was done in the United States. The United States Federal Census counts every resident in the United States, as mandated by the Constitution, every ten years. The information that the United States government collects varies from census to census. Several genealogy websites, such as ancestry.com, familysearch.org, and myheritage.com, provide access to U.S. Census Records. Some of these websites require you to pay for a subscription, so speak with a parent about them.

By law, U.S. Census records are sealed and unavailable to the public for 72 years after being completed. So you won't be able to find your parents in the U.S. Census, but you may be able to find your grandparents.

Some states in the United States decided to do their own census surveys, often during the years ending in 5. For example, you can find online New York State Census records from 1905, 1915, and 1925. These records can help you fill in the ten-year gaps between each Federal Census.

Pages from the 1925 New York State Census record listing the names of relatives of Stephen Cohen

Citizenship and Naturalization Records

Among the important records that many countries keep are documents about immigrants who became citizens of that country. In the United States, these records are kept by the National Archives and Records

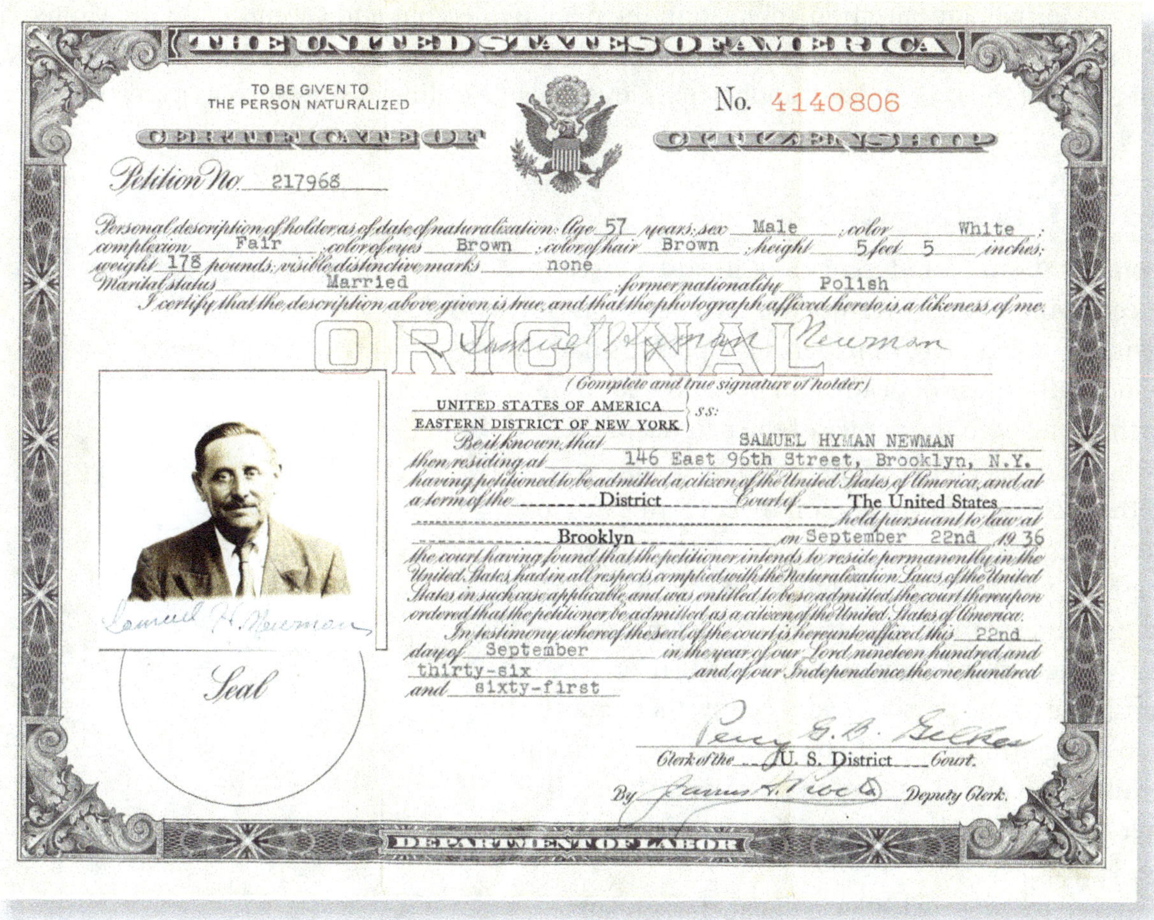

United States of America Certificate of Citizenship of a relative of Stephen Cohen: This one even includes a photograph

Administration (NARA), often called the "National Archives" for short. Many of NARA's documents are now digitized and online. You can learn a bit more about NARA's document collections by visiting its webpage at archives.gov.

Naturalization, or the process of becoming a citizen, might have taken your ancestors many years in the United States or another country. The records of these "naturalized" citizens can provide you with some useful clues:

- Their homeland
- The ship that they took to reach their new land
- Their occupation
- And more!

You might find a *Certificate of Citizenship* (example shown above), which contains valuable information, among old papers in your house. Even more

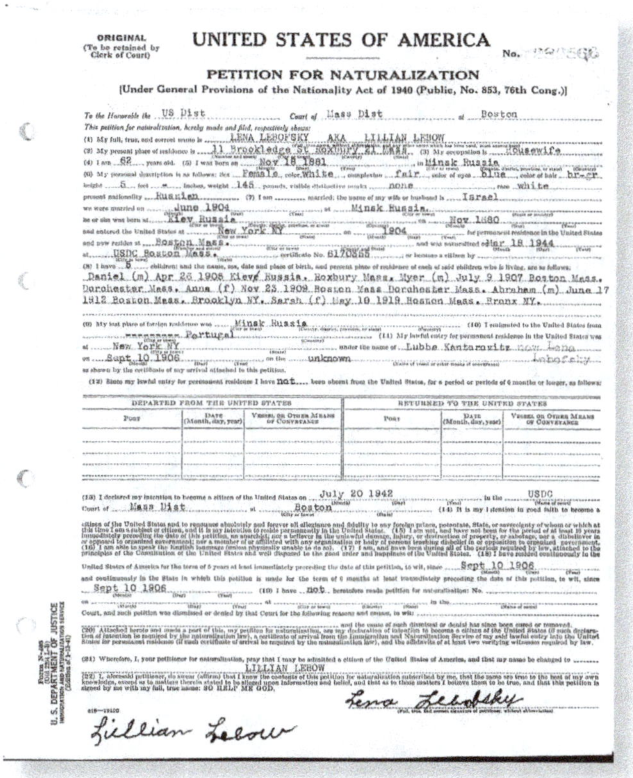

Petition for Naturalization

detailed is the initial naturalization application the person filled out and submitted to the United States government. Such an application to become a United States citizen is called a *Petition for Naturalization*. Images of many of these completed applications are available online at sites such as ancestry.com and familysearch.org.

✦ Death Certificates

A *death certificate* sounds scary, but it's just a piece of paper certifying to the government that a person is no longer living. On that piece of paper is the person's name, age, date of death, cause of death, and possibly the country of birth, along with the names of the parents of the person who died. If you like biology and medicine, you will find the medical information on these certificates to be interesting.

Sometimes you can find a death certificate at home, but usually you need to contact the city or town where your relative died, and request a copy of your relative's death certificate. If the person died recently, there may be restrictions on getting a copy if you aren't a direct descendant (a child, grandchild, etc.) of that person. About 50 years after the person's death, most of those restrictions no longer apply.

If you need to order a death certificate for a relative, search online for the government offices of the town or city where the person died, and call the town clerk for more information. Getting a death certificate usually costs a small amount of money, so ask a parent for help with ordering it.

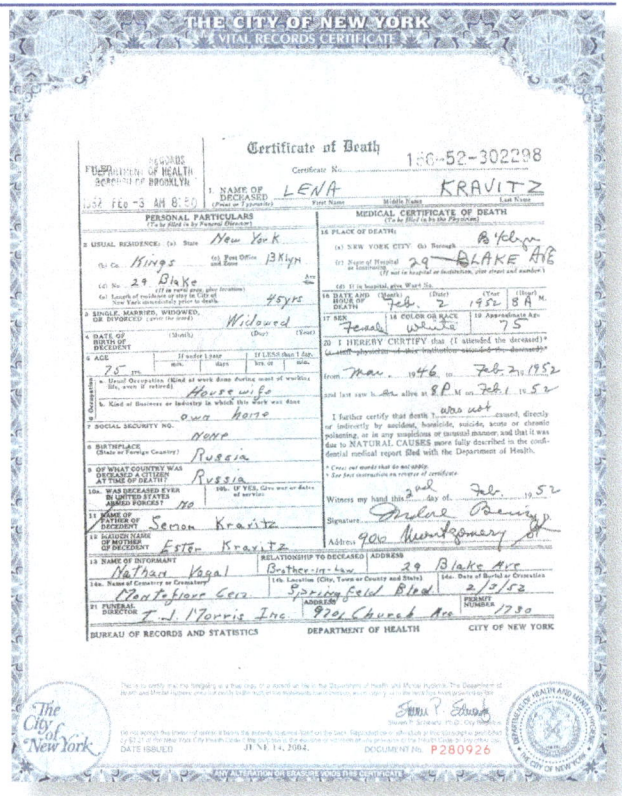

Certificate of Death obtained from New York City

✦ Birth Certificates

Like a death certificate, a *birth certificate* is an official paper from the local government describing the facts about a person's birth. A birth certificate tells the date, time, and address of the birth, the parents' names, and maybe the parents' ages and professions. Like a death certificate, you may need to be a direct descendant (a child, grandchild, etc.) of a person to get a recent birth certificate, and it will probably cost some money, so ask a parent for help with ordering it.

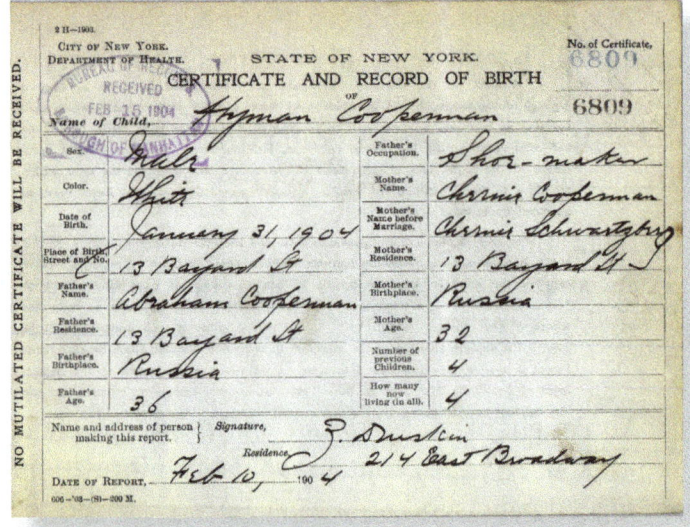

Birth certificate obtained from New York City

Go Back in Time   41

✡ *Marriage Certificates*

A *marriage certificate* gives the date and location of the wedding, names and ages of the couple getting married, possibly their parents' names, and the name of the person who performed the ceremony. Getting a copy costs money, and you have to write to the town where the couple was married, so once again, you'll need a parent to help you with ordering it. You might even be able to find such a certificate in your home.

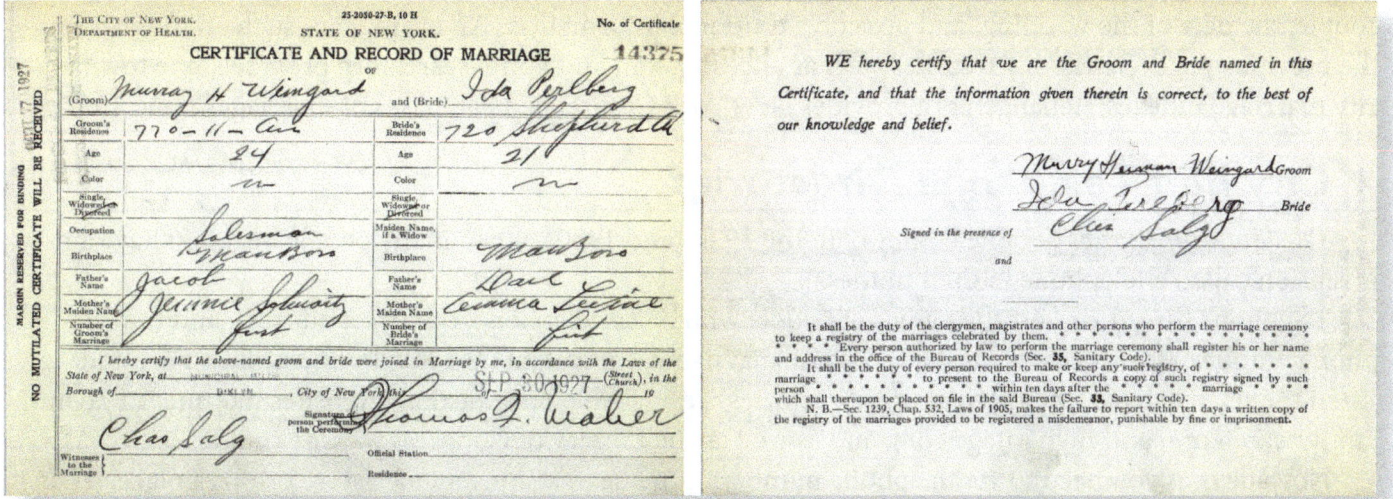

Front and back sides of a marriage certificate obtained from New York City

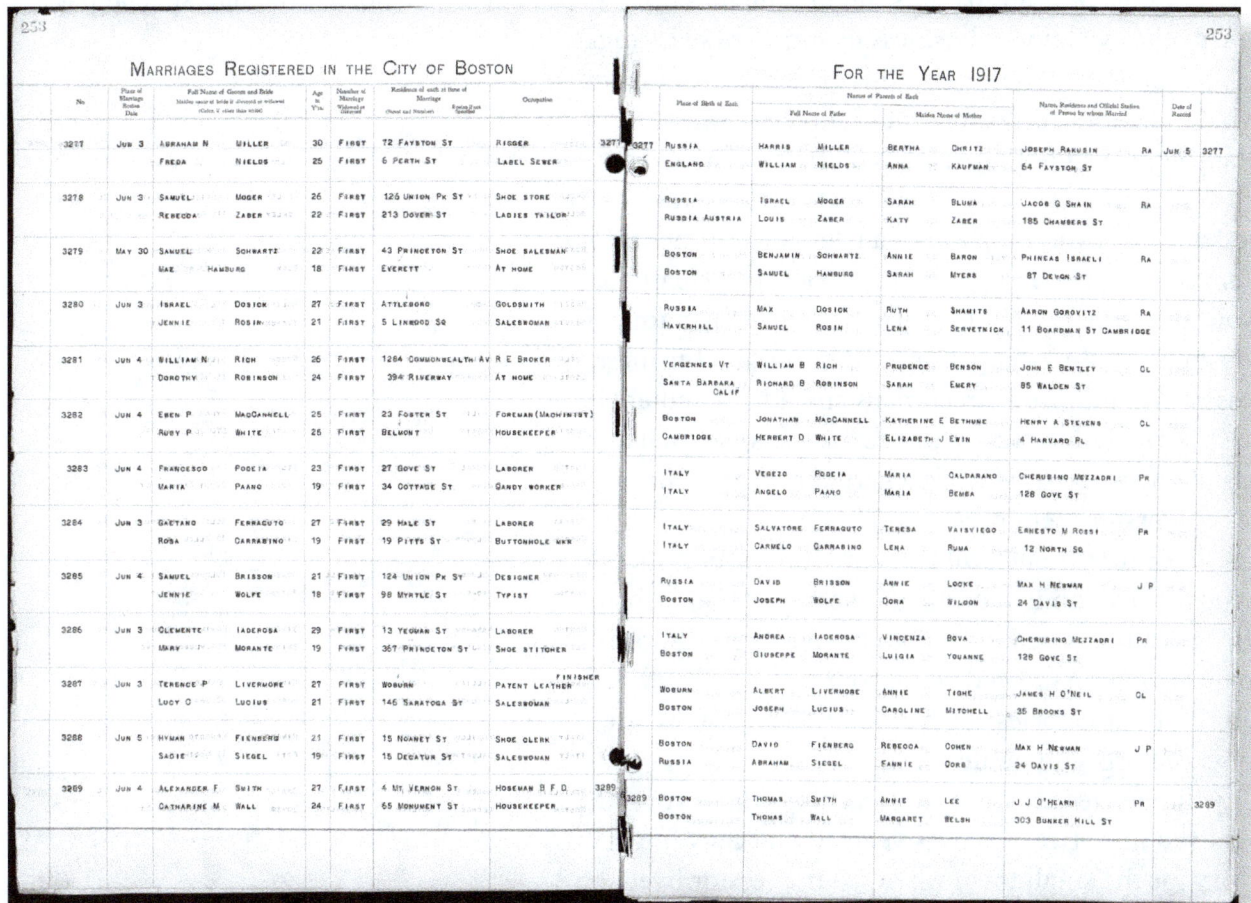

Pages from a 1917 marriage index for the city of Boston, Massachusetts, listing the names of relatives of Stephen Cohen

A marriage certificate is not the same thing as a *ketubah*, or Jewish marriage contract. The local government issues the marriage certificate, while the rabbi or cantor who performed the Jewish wedding ceremony completes the *ketubah* (more about *ketubot* in other chapters). If you can find a *ketubah* and decipher it, you will uncover a rich source of genealogy clues.

If a marriage certificate exists, you might be able to find it listed in a town's *marriage index*. The index, often an actual book or—in more modern times—a computer printout, generally provides the names of the couple, the date of the wedding, and possibly additional information. An example of such an index is on the previous page. Genealogy websites such as ancestry.com and familysearch.org provide some town and city marriage indexes; italiangen.org provides New York City-related databases of marriages up to 1937.

✡ City and Telephone Directories

Telephone directories became common in the 1920s and 1930s, when many people began to have a new invention called a telephone in their homes.

Telephone directories list the names of people who had a telephone, the street address, and the telephone number. If your relative had a more unusual name, this might be a way to figure out where and when the relative lived. Many telephone directories are available on genealogy websites like ancestry.com, familysearch.org, and myheritage.com, and as well as the Library of Congress website (guides.loc.gov).

Nowadays, if you need to get the phone number of the nearest convenience store or pizza place, it's as easy as a few clicks on a keyboard. Just one generation ago, however, it wasn't so simple.

Your parents or grandparents might remember big, paper telephone books that had special pages in the back printed in yellow for business listings. These listings were in alphabetical order according to the type of business. But what did people do before they had telephones?

Many cities printed directories of their citizens! These looked something like telephone directories, but they listed the person's profession instead of a telephone number. *City directories* were printed up until the 1960s. Information that you may find in city directories includes the name of the working person, occupation, and home and business addresses. You may find street maps and advertisements (which may include your ancestor's business), as well as listings of government officials, charitable organizations, houses of worship, cemeteries, and hotels.

These records are helpful for pinpointing your ancestor to a specific location in a particular year. Use that information to expand your search and seek out other local records that may have been created while your ancestor lived at that location. City directories can be found on ancestry.com, familysearch.org, and guides.loc.gov.

City directories are useful for tracking where your ancestors lived in-between census years. If you can't find a city directory for the small town where your ancestor lived, try checking directories of larger nearby cities to see whether your ancestor's smaller town might be included there.

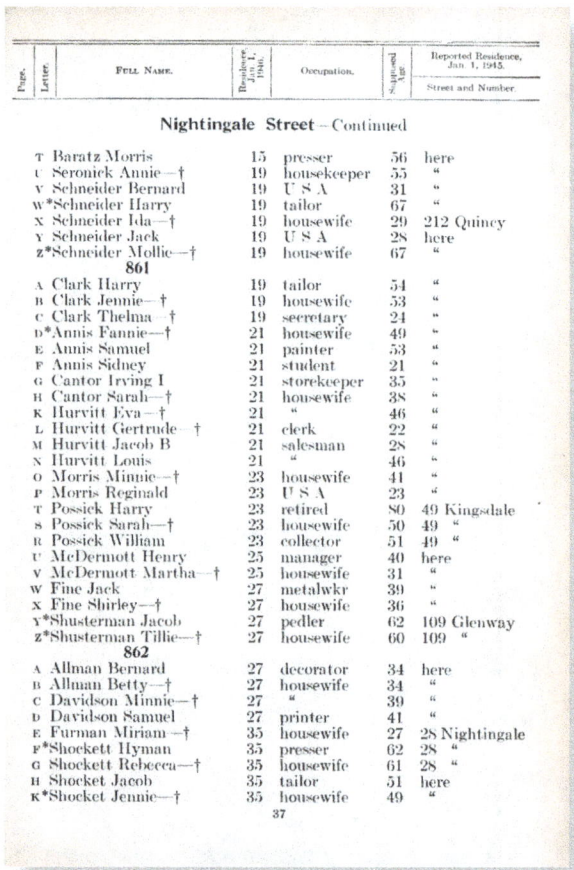

Page from a 1946 list of residents from Boston, Massachusetts

Many people share the same last name, so when you find your ancestor's name in a city directory, be sure to use other sources like censuses or family records to confirm that the address and occupation match that of your ancestor.

Take the time to look at the addresses and occupations of other people who share your ancestor's last name. You might find relatives who lived nearby or worked at the same type of job.

Since more men worked outside of the home than women in "the old days," you are more likely to find men listed in city directories than women. But you may find a widow listed in place of her deceased husband. Sometimes widows are listed in the directory with the abbreviation "wid" next to their names.

Stephen Cohen's relatives owned a grocery store in Detroit, Michigan in the late 1950s

✡ Professional Directories

Many professional organizations compiled books listing people with a particular job or profession. Doctors and lawyers, for example, are often listed in medical and legal directories. The *Martindale-Hubbell Law Directory* has listed lawyers in the United States since the 1800s. You may be able to find old *Martindale-Hubbell Law Directories* in university libraries. *Professional directories*—like telephone books—can help you pinpoint where a relative lived, and paint a picture of what life was like during that time period.

✡ Yearbooks and Autograph Books

Most high schools and colleges in North America have published *yearbooks*, listing people who were graduated that year, along with clubs, societies, and often teachers or professors. These books might even have some interesting comments written by friends to the owner of the yearbook. Some of these yearbooks are online, so you may be able to find relatives listed in a high school or college yearbook.

In years past, *autograph books* were popular. Students would bring the autograph book to school, usually at the end of the school year, and have classmates sign or "autograph" the pages of the book.

 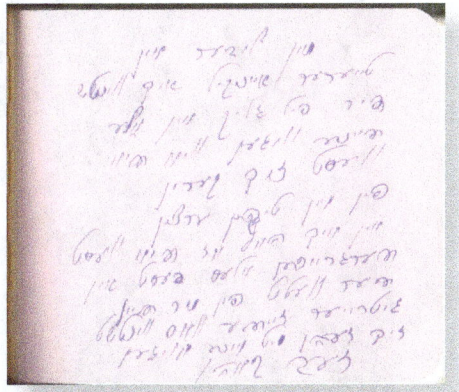 

Junior high school autograph book of Stephen Cohen's father: On one page of the autograph book, the author's great-grandfather wrote a Yiddish message, and signed it as "Zev," a rare proof of his Hebrew name

Page from a college yearbook with Stephen Cohen's father

Sometimes even family members would write something in the book. These books are not available online, but one of your relatives might have one stashed away somewhere and be willing to have you look at it.

✡ Military Records

Military records can provide valuable information about your family members who served in the military. Your search of military records will be easier if you know when and where the soldier served, and whether or not your relative was an officer. Military records may tell you where your relative lived, dates of birth and death, names and addresses of family members, and military rank.

If you speak with your grandparents and other family members, you may find that they can share with you newspaper articles, family stories, photo albums and scrapbooks, letters or diaries, photographs, and service medals.

The gravestones of a *veteran* (someone who has completed military service) can sometimes provide additional clues about that person's military service if you find out the name of the cemetery in which the veteran is buried. There are some cemeteries that allow only veterans to be buried there.

Caryn Alter's father at Fort Monmouth, New Jersey in the 1950s

You might even find military records for relatives who never actually served in the military. Millions of men, non-citizens and United States citizens alike, who were born between about 1872 and 1900 filled out World War I Draft Registration Cards. However, many of them were never actually called up for service. Even older men (born from 1877 to 1897) were registered in the United States during World War II (1939–1945), to determine their ability to work in factories or provide other services during a time of war. On these World War I and II Draft Registration Cards, you can see birth dates and birthplaces, addresses, names of nearest relatives and employers, and even signatures. Some genealogy websites have images of these registration cards.

During World War II, the National Jewish Welfare Board created files on over 100,000 American Jewish soldiers. These and other military records can be found online at websites like ancestry.com, familysearch.org, myheritage.com, and fold3.com.

If you have ancestors who fought in wars when they lived in other countries, you may be able to find information about their military service in those

Second from the right is Stephen Cohen's great-uncle during World War II

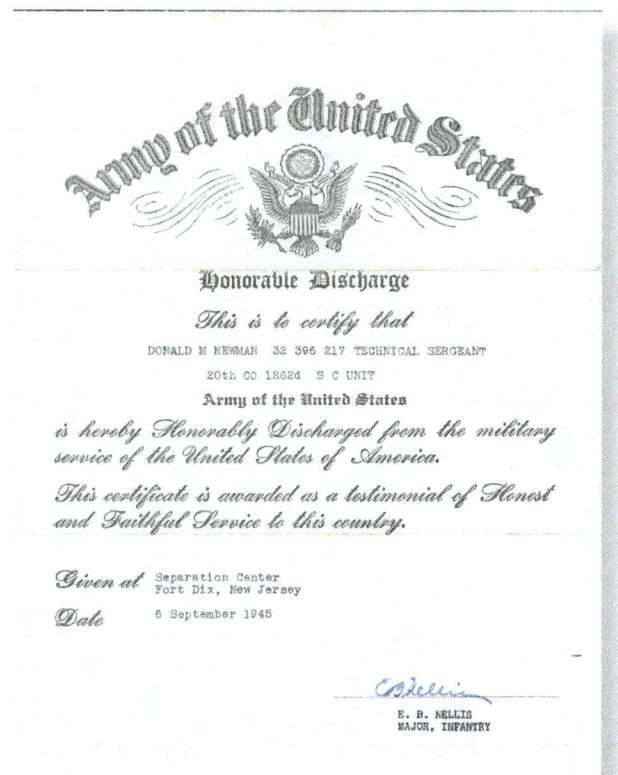

Front and back sides of a World War I Draft Registration Card

places as well. A research librarian at the library or a member of a local genealogy club may be able to help you with this search.

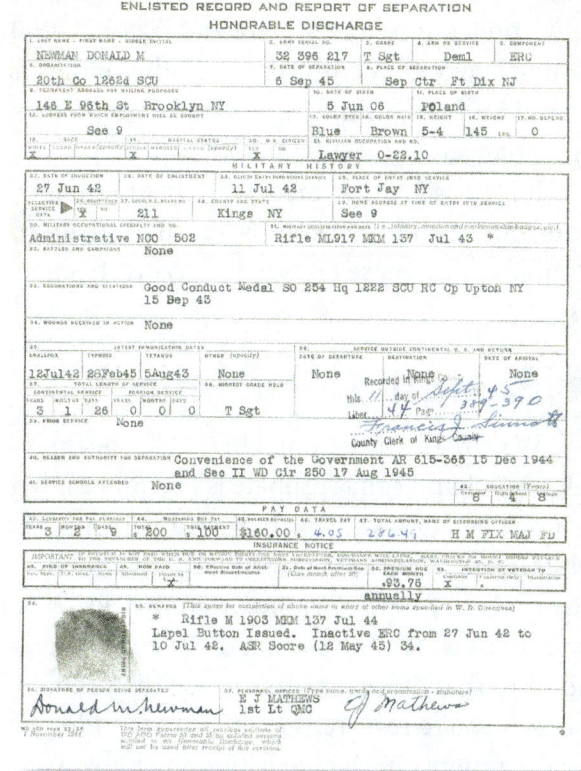

Front and back sides of an Honorable Discharge certificate from the United States Army after World War II

✸ Social Security Records

During the Great Depression in the 1930s, the United States set up the Social Security Administration to provide a kind of insurance for retired people. Most workers (but not all, such as railroad workers) were required to register for Social Security. You can get copies of completed applications for Social Security for people who are no longer living. There are United States Social Security Death Index (SSDI) records from 1935 through recent years on a number of websites.

Social Security application obtained from the United States Social Security Administration

Social Security applications, available from the U.S. government's Social Security Administration, are useful because many immigrants wrote their birthday and place of birth on their application, along with their mother's *maiden name* (the last name of the mother before marrying). Since it was an official government application, the person applying for Social Security had to sign the document, so you will see your relative's actual signature! (Getting this record does cost money, so ask a parent to help you.) The Social Security Applications and Claims Index, 1936–2007, available online at ancestry.com, also includes name changes. This would be valuable information if a woman got married and changed her last name.

It is possible that incorrect information could have been entered into a person's Social Security record, so double-check these facts with records from other sources.

✸ Probate Documents

We already mentioned in the "Genealogy Techniques" chapter that probate is the process by which a judge decides what to do with a person's belongings after death, if there is no will. All documents relating to the probate process are stored in the clerk's office of the county in which the person died. You can go with an adult to that office, and ask to see the probate file for the person you're researching. If there is a file, there should be documents in the file listing the person's nearest relatives (parents, siblings, children; nieces and nephews if no children) and their addresses. Making copies of the

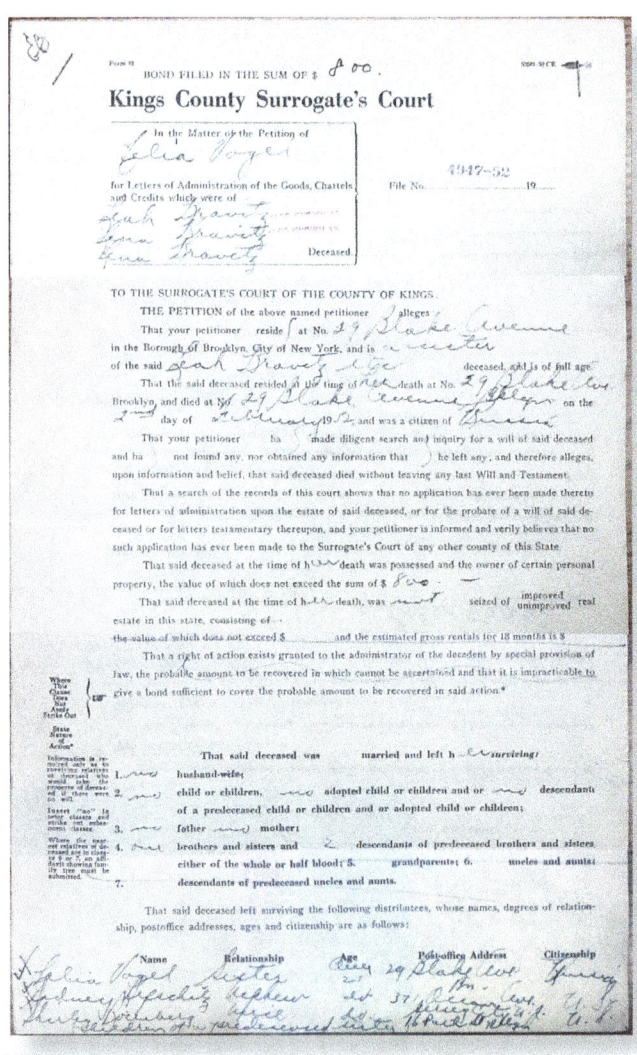

1952 probate record from Kings County Surrogate Court in Brooklyn, New York for Stephen Cohen's cousin: It lists the deceased person's nearest relatives and their addresses

papers in the file may cost money. You might be permitted to take photographs of the papers with your cell phone's camera.

✶ Patents

Inventor alert!

Was your relative an inventor or engineer? Perhaps a family member created something new that was patented. This means that the government officially recognizes this person as the creator. There is a searchable database of worldwide patents at patents.google.com. If your relative had an unusual last name (surname), it should be especially easy to find their invention in the database. Who knows? Maybe someday you, too, can be permanently recognized in the patent listings if you dream up a new invention!

Stephen Cohen's cousin patented some electronic inventions

✶ Newspapers

Online searching of newspapers makes finding articles about your relatives a lot easier. Search for newspapers that were published in the communities in which your relatives lived. Newspapers often published birth notices, wedding announcements (and sometimes whether a marriage license was obtained), and obituaries (death announcements). These are valuable records because they provide important facts about your relatives including ages, dates, names of other family members, and interests.

Don't be surprised if you do a search and discover that a relative was interviewed for a story, or was featured in an article for doing something worthwhile for the community. Perhaps your relative was even a reporter or wrote a letter to the editor of the newspaper. If your relative ran a business, there might have been an advertisement for that business in the newspaper.

There are a number of websites with collections of newspapers that are searchable. If your relative lived in New York City or the State of New York, there are some

"Vacation Personals" column from the September 4, 1921 edition of the *Brooklyn Standard Union* newspaper: One person mentioned is Mrs. Helen Rockmuller, a relative of Stephen Cohen

websites like bklyn.newspapers.com, fultonhistory.com, and help.nytimes.com dedicated to newspapers specifically from that area. General newspaper databases like genealogybank.com and newspaperarchive.com are also available, but may cost money to access. Ask a parent about subscribing to such databases.

If your relative lived in a small town, almost anything could have passed as news: One of the authors found newspaper reports that cousins contracted poison ivy, and other articles about relatives entertaining guests! (Those must have been slow news days!)

Don't forget to search the local Jewish newspapers as well. In these newspapers, you can find birth announcements, wedding announcements, obituaries, and bar or bat mitzvah announcements. Major Jewish newspapers have been published in New York, New Jersey, Houston, Philadelphia, Cleveland, Detroit, and many other places.

Tel Aviv University created an amazing database (nli.org.il/en) of digitized Jewish newspapers from around the world in Hebrew, Yiddish, Polish, Russian, French, and other languages. You can peruse the *Forverts* (Yiddish, based in New York), *Davar* (Hebrew, based in Israel), *OJCZYZNA* (Polish, based in Poland), *La América* (Djudezmo, based in New York), *La Liberté* (French, based in Tangiers, Morocco), and *The Occident and American Jewish Advocate* (English, based in Philadelphia), among many, many others. Perhaps your relatives are mentioned in one or more of these periodicals.

A donation announcement from Refeyl Leyb Gordon of Čekiškė (now in Lithuania), in the Hebrew newspaper *HaMelitz*, April 18, 1899: Mr. Gordon was a relative of Stephen Cohen

If your family is from Germany, don't forget to search jewishgen.org's database of the German-Jewish newspaper *Aufbau*, published in New York City. This newspaper was printed partly in English and partly in German and, in addition to news, included birth, marriage, and death announcements.

What kinds of documents from the past can you find? List some relatives, the documents that referred to them, and some new facts you learned from these documents.

Relative	Document(s) Mentioning Your Relative	Facts you learned from the document(s)

Mysteries in the Cemetery

You might think that cemeteries are creepy and scary. But they can actually provide a treasure trove of information about your ancestors. Learning how to understand the words and symbols on a gravestone is like solving a puzzle: Each piece gets you one step closer to seeing the "big picture."

If you do have the opportunity to visit a Jewish cemetery to research your relatives, your family will likely be very proud of you and your interest in your heritage. It's even a mitzvah to visit the cemetery and think about your ancestors.

Some Jews, including children, who are *Kohanim* (descendants of the High Priests from biblical times), have a tradition of not visiting cemeteries. If you follow this tradition, you may want to ask another person to visit the cemetery to record for you the information found on the gravestones.

✡ What's on a Gravestone?

A gravestone is called a *matzeva* in Hebrew. Jewish gravestones often have the following information:

- Jewish name of the deceased (person who died)
- Father's Jewish name (and sometimes the mother's)
- Hebrew date of death
- Symbols that represent *Kohen* or *Levi*
- Carvings on the gravestone that have something to do with the person's interests or life
- Important abbreviations in Hebrew

Not all gravestones have all of these items, but most have at least some of them. The more information the *matzeva* has, the more clues you'll get about your ancestors!

✡ A Real Example

Let's examine a typical gravestone, a real one from one of the authors' families:

You can guess that this is probably a husband (Michael Newman) on the left, and his wife (Beckie Newman) on the right. Often husbands and wives buy joint cemetery plots to be buried together. But this is not always the case. Sometimes the plots are separated because of space restrictions or even for religious reasons: Some Jews believe that men and women shouldn't be next to each other, even in death.

✦ Let's Decode Some Symbols

At the top center is a "Jewish star," or *magen david* (Shield of David), which is a typical modern Jewish symbol.

On the left is a pair of hands held so that there is a space between two groups of fingers. This is how Jews who are descended from *Kohanim* (the High Priests from biblical times) hold their hands and bless the congregation to this very day. Therefore, the "pair of hands" symbol on this gravestone indicates that Michael Newman was a *Kohen*.

On the right is a sketch of a menorah (even though it has only five branches). This doesn't indicate Hanukkah—that menorah has nine branches! No, this is a symbol of Beckie Newman being a woman, because women typically light the Sabbath candles in the Jewish tradition.

Let's read some Hebrew now. If you do know Hebrew, follow along. If you can't read Hebrew, we are here to help you.

The top line on the gravestone, just under the Jewish star, has five Hebrew letters like this: ת'נ'צ'ב'ה'.

This is an abbreviation that stands for "May his/her soul be bound up in the bond of eternal life," and is found on many gravestones.

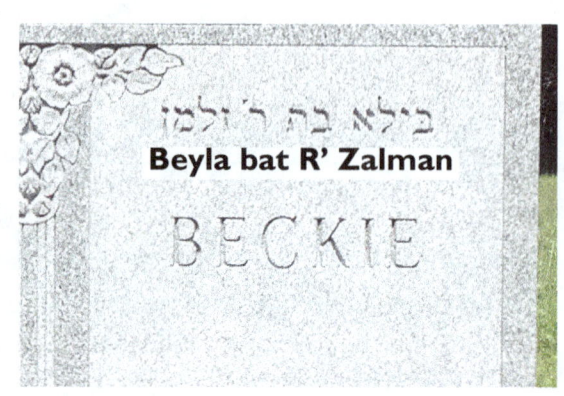

Leonard Nimoy, who played Spock in the original "Star Trek" series, used the Kohen symbol as his inspiration for the Vulcan greeting.

✦ The Grave on the Right

Now let's look at the grave on the right, for Beckie Newman.

The Hebrew says *Beyla bat R' Zalman*, which means "Beyla daughter of Mr. Zalman." Now we know that Beckie's Jewish name was Beyla, and that she was the daughter of a man named Zalman.

Here's a mystery that even Stephen Cohen, Beckie's relative, hasn't yet solved: Why, if Beckie died in 1969, is there no information carved below her name on the gravestone?

Sometimes there might even be mistakes on the gravestones, because the information on the gravestones is usually provided by the relatives of the person who died. The gravestone of Caryn Alter's grandfather had to be corrected because it was noticed that part of his Jewish name was spelled incorrectly.

✡ Myth-Busting Alert!!

Some people think that the abbreviation ׳ר (R') means "rabbi," but it is actually an abbreviation for "*Reb,*" which means "Mr." There are many abbreviations in Hebrew to designate a rabbi, most of which include the letter *mem* (מ) in an abbreviation, that may stand for *moreinu* ("our teacher" in Hebrew). One example is the abbreviation מו״ה, which stands for *moreinu harav* (our teacher the master/rabbi), often indicating a rabbi. There is no *mem* on Beckie's gravestone before her father's name, so her father was probably not a rabbi.

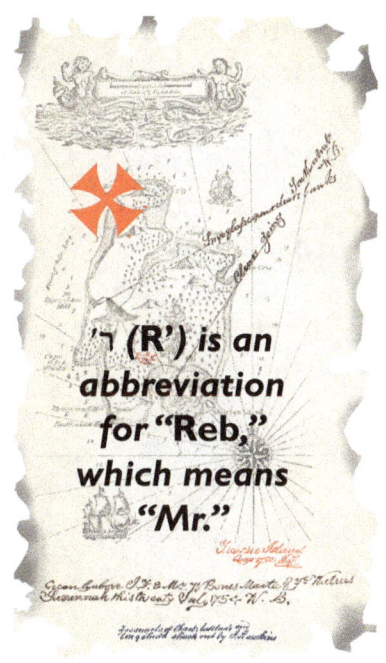

׳ר (R') is an abbreviation for "Reb," which means "Mr."

✡ The Grave on the Left

Now let's look at the grave on the left, for Michael Newman:
The first line under the hands is *ba'ali hayakar*, or "my beloved hus-

My beloved husband
Micha'el b'r Avraham haKohen
6 Tishri 5722

band." No other family is mentioned, so we can guess that he had no children, and any siblings have already died. The second line is *Micha'el b'r Avraham haKohen*, or "Michael, son of Mr. Avraham the Kohen."

Now we learn that Michael Newman's Jewish name was *Micha'el*, and that his father was *Avraham*, a member of the *Kohanim*. This explains the "hands" symbol on the top of the gravestone (see page 50). As mentioned above, *b'r* is an abbreviation for *ben reb*, that is, "son of Mr."

The third line is "6 Tishri 5722," which is the Hebrew date on which Michael died. (Years in the Hebrew calendar are traditionally counted by starting with the creation of the world.) But wait a second: If there is no "6" or "5722" on the tombstone, how did we get that date?

Guess what? Hebrew letters can also stand for numbers!

✡ Become a Decoding Detective!

Have you learned about Roman numerals in school? What is this number?
MDCCLXXVI
1000 + 500 + 100 + 100 + 50 + 10 + 10 + 5 + 1, or 1776
All Americans know this number as the common or secular year of the USA's independence.

Hebrew numerals work the same way as Roman numerals. This table goes from right to left—like the Hebrew alphabet—because you read Hebrew numbers from right to left:

Yod	Tet	Chet	Zayin	Vav	Hey	Dalet	Gimel	Bet	Aleph
י	ט	ח	ז	ו	ה	ד	ג	ב	א
10	9	8	7	6	5	4	3	2	1

Cryptology alert!

So the number 6 (as in the 6th of Tishri) is represented as a *vav* all by itself, ו. To make 13, you put the *yod* together with the *gimel*: יג, or 10 + 3.

(But you can't put together *yod* and *hey* to make 15, or *yod* and *vav* to make 16, because those letter combinations spell out the name of God, and Jews avoid writing God's name. Instead, 9 + 6 = 15 too, so we can write 15 as טו. And 9 + 7 = 16, so we write 16 as טז.)

What do you do about larger numbers?

Don't mix up ח and ה!

Kuf	Tsadi	Pey	Ayin	Samech	Nun	Mem	Lamed	Kaf
ק	צ	פ	ע	ס	נ	מ	ל	כ
100	90	80	70	60	50	40	30	20

To write the 24th of a month, we use *kaf* and *dalet*, 20 + 4: כד.

For even bigger numbers:

Tav	Shin	Resh
ת	ש	ר
400	300	200

For thousands, we go back to the beginning of the Hebrew alphabet, but then add a *geresh*, which is a kind of Hebrew apostrophe, to show that it's a smaller number multiplied by a thousand:

Yod	Tet	Chet	Zayin	Vav	Hey	Dalet	Gimel	Bet	Aleph
י׳	ט׳	ח׳	ז׳	ו׳	ה׳	ד׳	ג׳	ב׳	א׳
10 000	9000	8000	7000	6000	5000	4000	3000	2000	1000

2222 is therefore 2000 + 200 + 20 + 2, or ב׳רכב.
(There is no "zero" in this system, which was invented before people in the Middle East had ever heard of a zero.)

Write the secular year 1776 using Hebrew letters. (We'll give you the first letter to help you get started.)

א׳

Now write the year on Michael Newman's tombstone, 5722, in Hebrew letters:

To write the year 5722, you should have started with a *hey* with a *geresh*, ה׳. But on the tombstone, there is only תשכב, or 722. Usually the Hebrew letter representing the number 5000 is omitted because the year is most likely in the 5000s anyway.

Both answers are on page 60.

Finally, for the full translation of the date on the grave, we add the Hebrew month of *Tishri*. The Jewish year has twelve months:

Number	Name of Month	Hebrew spelling
1	Nisan	ניסן
2	Iyar	אייר
3	Sivan	סיון
4	Tammuz	תמוז
5	Av	אב
6	Elul	אלול
7	Tishri	תשרי
8	Marcheshvan (or Cheshvan)	מרחשון (or חשון)
9	Kislev	כסלו
10	Tevet	טבת
11	Shevat	שבט
12	Adar (Adar II)	אדר (אדר ב׳)

This is also useful for deciphering a ketubah!

Sometimes an extra *Adar* is added to the year—as you see on line 12 of the Jewish months chart—because the Hebrew calendar doesn't exactly match our 365-day secular calendar. This way, Passover remains in the spring each year (at least in the Northern Hemisphere of the Earth). The Hebrew calendar is based on phases of the moon, adjusted to match the sun.

Hebrew written on gravestones almost never includes vowels, which is why we didn't include vowels in the table of months. Even if you can't read Hebrew, it helps to be able to recognize the months, so you can read a *matzeva*. If you need help with converting a Hebrew date to a date in the Gregorian or Common calendar, you will find the website hebcal.com to be very useful.

✡ Some Other Symbols on Gravestones

- **Pitcher:** Indicates that the person is a *Levi*. Sometimes the pitcher is shown pouring water into a bowl, as the *Levi'im* did in the Great Temple in Jerusalem in ancient days when they were in charge of cleaning the hands of the Temple High Priest, or *Kohen*.
- **Broken branch or tree stump:** Indicates that the person's life was "cut short," that is, the person died too young.
- **Book:** Indicates a learned or educated person.
- **Carvings of animals:** Sometimes a person's name may be related to the word for an animal. *Dov* means "bear" in Hebrew, so a bear symbol may mean the person's name was *Dov* (or *Ber* in Yiddish). *Tsvi/Tzvi* and *Naftali* in Hebrew (and *Hirsh/Hersh* in Yiddish) mean "deer." *Ari* or *Arye* in Hebrew (and *Leyb* in Yiddish) mean "lion." *Tzipora* in Hebrew (and *Feygl* in Yiddish) mean "bird."

Here are examples of interesting carvings on gravestones, photographed by Caryn Alter in an old Jewish cemetery in Ukraine.

✡ More Things to Learn from Gravestones

Often the abbreviation פ״נ (*Pey Nun*), which means "here lies," is carved near the top of a gravestone.

Sometimes there is a small porcelain photograph of the person who died attached to the gravestone. If the gravestone of one of your relatives has one of these photographs, you will be able to see what that person looked like. Some gravestones have a picture of the person who died carved right into the stone.

Often the gravestone mentions if the person had family members, like sisters or brothers, children, grandchildren, and so on. If the gravestone doesn't mention children, the person probably didn't have any sons or daughters. This can be an important clue when tracing your family.

Here are gravestones for a husband and wife with Hebrew poetry. The first letters of each line spell out the names of the deceased. We color-coded the Hebrew to match the English translation. Also underneath the carvings of vines is the abbreviation פ׳נ, and above the English names is the abbreviation ת׳נ׳צ׳ב׳ה׳.

✡ The Weird Hebrew Letter

Here is a letter you likely never learned in Hebrew school, but might find on a gravestone, especially that of a Sephardic Jew: אל. This is a combination of the aleph א and lamed ל. Such combinations, called *ligatures*, were invented in the Middle Ages, and are common in Arabic, but also in old European manuscripts. For example, you may know that the symbol & (an *ampersand*) means the word "and," but it is actually a ligature of e plus t (the Latin word *et*, meaning "and"). The *aleph-lamed* ligature אל is the same idea. An example of this ligature on a gravestone would be אליעזר, the Hebrew name Eliezer with the *aleph* and *lamed* together.

✡ Landsmanshaftn *and Mutual Aid Societies*

Landsmanshaft is a Yiddish word that means "association of people from the same geographical area." Most *landsmanshaftn* (plural) were organized in the late 1800s and early 1900s by people who came from the same town or region in Europe. These societies, called mutual aid or benefit societies, provided social and financial support to new immigrants.

Other kinds of societies included those that were associated with a social movement or synagogue, and "ladies auxiliary" societies. Some were even set up for people with the same job or profession.

Landsmanshaftn often bought land in cemeteries so that the graves of all the society's members would be in the same section of the cemetery. This means that if you have relatives buried in such a society plot, they may have come from the town for which that society was named. There were some exceptions, but generally most people buried in the society's section of the cemetery had some connection to the society.

A *landsmanshaft* plot may have a large archway at the entrance, with names of the founding members carved into it. Some of these names may be your relatives, so be on the lookout!

Here are some names of *landsmanshaftn* and mutual aid societies in which relatives of Caryn Alter and Stephen Cohen are buried, and the people served by each one:

Society	Origin of Its Members	People Served
Lenyin & Lachwer Benevolent Association	Lenino and Lakhva, in Belarus	People from the two nearby towns of Lenino and Lakhva, in southern Belarus
Berdichever Independent Benevolent Association	Berdichev, Ukraine	People from Berdichev, a city in Ukraine
Benevolent Society Sons of Aaron Solomon Govorow	Goworowo, Poland	People from Goworowo, a *shtetl* in northeastern Poland. There was a dispute between some people in the first society, so a group split off and created a second one!
Govorover Young Men's Benevolent Association	Goworowo, Poland	
Jewish Postal Workers Welfare League	New York City	For Jews who worked for the U.S. Postal Service
Yampoler Volyner Benevolent Society	Yampol, Ukraine	People from Yampol, a *shtetl* in the province of Volhynia, Ukraine

Are any of your relatives buried in a *landsmanshaft* or mutual aid society plot? Talk to older relatives to find out. List the societies, and what sort of people they serve. If you need more room, copy the page and staple it here.

Society	Original Town/Region of Its Members	People Served

Landsmanshaftn haven't completely vanished. There are still a few of these organizations, such as the David-Horodoker Organization in Detroit, Michigan, which connects people whose ancestors came from the *shtetl* of Davyd-Haradok in southern Belarus. There are a number of *landsmanshaftn* around the world for the city of Łódź, in Poland. Do some online searches to see which societies might be related to your family history.

Mysteries in the Cemetery 57

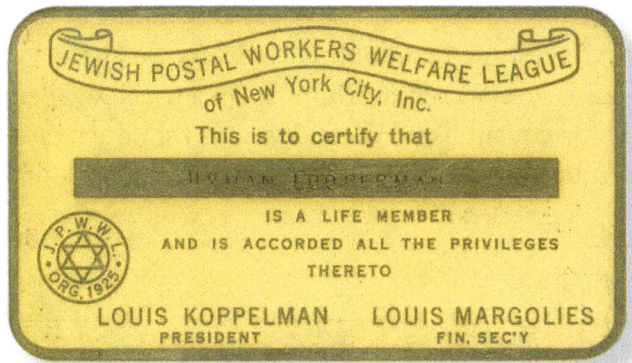

Brass membership card owned by a relative of Stephen Cohen (the relative was a postal clerk)

65th-anniversary book published by the David-Horodoker Organization in Detroit, Michigan in 2002

✦ Be Respectful at the Cemetery

There is nothing to be afraid of in a cemetery. It is usually a peaceful place with grass and trees and a lot of history.

If you go, be respectful of the grave, for it is the final "home" of your relative. Try not to walk on the grave. Don't take grave-rubbings by placing a large sheet of paper on the gravestone and rubbing a crayon over the carvings to copy the design—this can damage some soft stones.

If you were lucky enough to know this person when they were still alive, think about all the good things that this person taught you. If you didn't know the person, you can still try to imagine how that person may have influenced your family. Consider that genealogy has made you think about that person's influence. And leave a small stone or pebble on the gravestone, as a traditional Jewish symbol that you took the time to visit your relative.

✦ Finding the Cemetery

Suppose you or your parents don't know which cemetery to visit. There is online help for you!

There are websites like findagrave.com and billiongraves.com that provide general information about cemeteries and gravestones, and websites like jewishgen.org/databases/Cemetery, mitzvatemet.com/en/burials, and beheshtieh.com that provide information specifically about Jewish cemeteries and gravestones. Some websites may even provide photographs of the gravestones, when available. There is a growing database of burials in Jewish cemeteries from around the world called the JewishGen Online Worldwide Burial Registry (JOWBR). Many Jewish genealogical societies encourage their members to record all local burials for this online database. Individual cemeteries may even have their own online search engines for gravestones.

Although *cremation* (burning a dead body into ashes) has not been part of the Jewish tradition, it may still occur. Stephen Cohen got seemingly conflicting accounts from relatives and newspaper articles about the burial or cremation of a cousin. After finding the cousin's gravestone in an online cemetery database, the author searched the online database specifically for the Fresh Ponds crematorium in Queens, New York at italiangen.org/databases/search/?db=crematory and found his cousin listed there. It seems that the cousin *was* cremated, and his ashes were buried in the cemetery. You should keep this possibility in the back of your mind as you do your research.

✡ Decode a Relative's Gravestone!

Ask your parents or another family member to take you to a cemetery where there are gravestones for your relatives. Remember to bring your cell phone. Go to the main cemetery office and ask the clerk to give you a map showing you where the gravestones are located. Take clear pictures of the graves and staple a copy of each photo onto this page.

Fill in the information on this chart for a relative's gravestone. If you visit the gravestones of several relatives, make as many copies of this chart as you need, and staple them onto this page.

Name in English (if stated)	
Jewish name	
Father's Jewish name (and mother's, if stated)	
Secular date of death	
Hebrew date of death	
Names of relatives (if stated)	
Symbols on the gravestone	
Any other useful information on the gravestone	

Answers to the questions on page 53:

| The secular year 1776 | א׳תשעו | 1000 + 400 + 300 + 70 + 6 |
| Michael Newman's year of death (5722) | ה׳תשכב | 5000 + 400 + 300 + 20 + 2 |

Clues from Beyond the United States

Although Israel and the United States have Jewish populations that number in the millions, other countries around the world also have sizeable Jewish populations. The languages spoken in these countries may vary, but some basic detective skills will help you track down family members—no matter where in the world they have lived or currently live.

Here are tips for researching your Jewish relatives in some of the countries that currently have larger Jewish populations (There is extensive information available online about Jewish history in other countries not mentioned here):

✡ British Commonwealth

There are many Jews who are residents of lands outside the United States where English is spoken, particularly Canada, the United Kingdom (UK), Australia, and South Africa (all part of the *British Commonwealth*). The British Commonwealth is an organization of "member states" or countries that generally were once territories of the former British Empire. Many records exist to help you search for family members who live or lived in these countries.

For Jews who emigrated to Canada, most arrived in the late 19th and early 20th centuries, and now live in the areas around Montréal, Toronto, and Winnipeg.

The first Jewish emigrants to Australia arrived as prisoners in 1788, but the community gradually grew throughout the 19th century. As of 2023, Australia had the largest proportion of Holocaust survivors of any country except Israel.

In South Africa, most of the Jews are descended from Litvaks (Jews of northeastern Europe), who also arrived in the late 19th and early 20th centuries.

Though there were Jews in Britain in medieval times, King Edward I drove them out in 1290. Under the leadership of Oliver Cromwell in the 1600s, Sephardic Jews began to trickle back into Britain, where they make up a large percentage of the current Jewish population.

Different countries within the British Commonwealth have different laws and customs, which will be important for your genealogy "detective work."

"British" refers to the entire United Kingdom (UK) or Britain. "English" refers only to England, one of the countries in the UK.

Jewish and General Records for the British Commonwealth

Jewishgen.org has records from the countries in the British Commonwealth. Additionally, there are databases with Jewish records specific to the United Kingdom (JewishGen's Jewish Communities and Records - United Kingdom Database), Canada (The Canadian Jewish Heritage Network at cjhn.ca and the Jewish Genealogical Society of Montréal at jgs-montreal.org), Australia (Australian Jewish Genealogical Society at ajgs.org.au), and South Africa (SA Jewish Rootsbank at jewishroots.uct.ac.za).

For information on census records, citizenship and naturalization, deaths, births, and marriages, the following government websites may be helpful: United Kingdom (nationalarchives.gov.uk), Canada (library-archives.canada.ca), Australia (naa.gov.au), and South Africa (nationalarchives.gov.za). Some genealogy websites also have these types of records.

Census Records

Most countries take regular censuses of their populations. In Canada, census records are arranged by province or territory. These records include information similar to the United States Census records, but may also include religion.

Canada has restrictions on who is allowed to view the information contained in censuses taken less than 90 years before the current date. The first national census was taken in Lower Canada (now the Province of Québec) in 1825, though there were counts taken as early as the 1600s. There was an 1842 census, and then, from 1851 to 1901, censuses were taken every ten years. Library and Archives Canada (library-archives.canada.ca) has digitized and placed online many of these records.

The United Kingdom (England, Wales, Scotland, Ireland until its independence, and Northern Ireland) has had a national census nearly every ten years (except for 1941) since 1801. Other partial censuses have been done on some of the five-year anniversaries in-between the every-ten-year censuses. Many British census records are now available online at nationalarchives.gov.uk.

Australia held its first census in 1911, with more taken at various intervals through 1961. After that, censuses were recorded every five years. The National Archives of Australia (naa.gov.au) has online census records through 1921.

In South Africa, the first complete national census was taken in 1911, and repeated every five years. Unfortunately, most census records were destroyed except for general summaries, with the exception of those from a few scattered towns.

Citizenship and Naturalization Records

Records of naturalization in Canada through 1951 are stored at the Library and Archives Canada, and can be found online through its website.

In the UK, an 1844 Act of Parliament allowed non-citizens (aliens) to become British citizens. Certificates of naturalization from 1870 until about 1911 are available by visiting the National Archives in London or by exploring its website. The National Archives of Australia has citizenship records, including naturalization certificates, on its website. Many South African naturalizations can be found using the South African Jewish Rootsbank web page.

Death Certificates

Canada puts death certificates under the control of the individual provinces. Information on where to find Canadian death certificates can be found online.

After July 1, 1837, England's General Register Office (GRO) kept a copy of all death records, and allows you to search its index for free (gro.gov.uk). There are several other websites with indexes of death records for England and Wales.

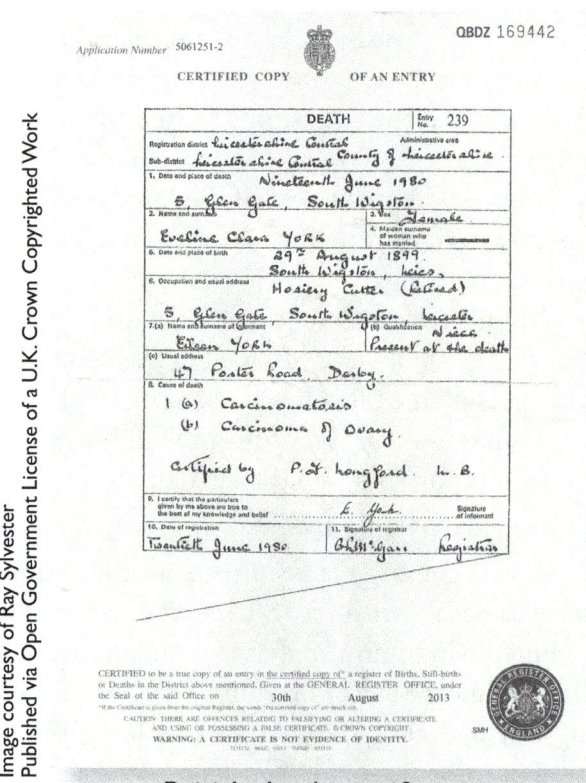

British death certificate

For Australia, there are websites available that provide death records arranged by territory. The Australian Jewish Genealogical Society also has compiled a list of some death records.

Additionally, a number of South African death indexes from 1895–1972 are available online.

Birth Certificates

The Jewish Genealogical Society of Montréal has indexed many Province of Québec birth records, called "Drouin" records. In general, each province controls its own death records. Many of these records are available online.

In the United Kingdom, the GRO keeps records of all births on its searchable online index.

In Australia, each territory compiles its own lists of birth records, which are available online.

In South Africa, the South African Jewish Rootsbank website contains indexes of births.

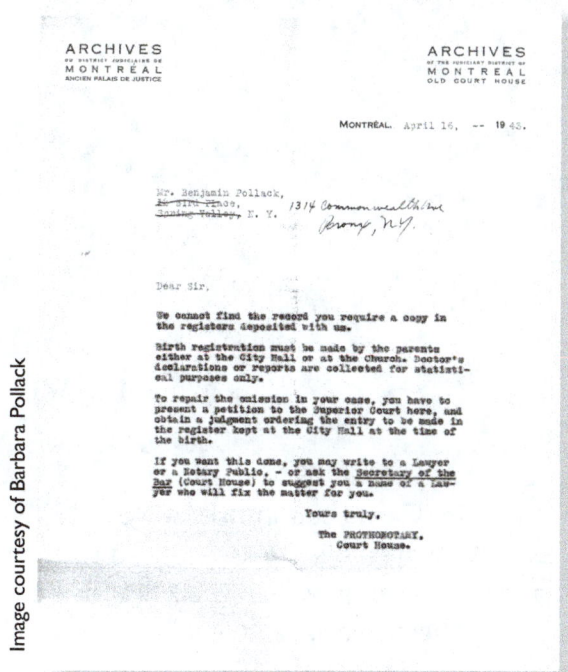

Official reply to Stephen Cohen's cousin who was born in Montréal and trying to get his birth record

Marriage Certificates

Although many Canadian marriage records are now available on online databases, you may have to contact each province, or a genealogical society in that province, for more guidance.

In the United Kingdom, marriage records, just like birth and death records, are kept by the GRO. Some of these records are available online and on microfilm. Older London synagogues such as the Bevis Marks Synagogue, built in 1701, can have records stretching back hundreds of years (Search JewishGen's United Kingdom Database and JewishGen's Sephardic Collection for marriage records of the Bevis Marks Synagogue).

In Australia, you have to contact the individual territories for marriage records.

South African Jewish Rootsbank is a valuable resource for South African Jewish marriages.

Other Records

Many Jewish communities in the British Commonwealth published annual or regular guides highlighting the local "influencers." The website freebmd.org.uk is updated regularly and has British civil records. South African Jews published *The South African Jewish Year Book*, and you can find all sorts of cool biographical information about selected South African Jews in these volumes.

South African Jewish military records and emigration records are searchable through South African Jewish Rootsbank.

When census records are difficult to get, you can try searching lists of eligible voters. The Province of Ontario in Canada created voter lists of various towns, which are available on genealogy websites. Women did not have the right to vote during the 19th century, so you won't find women listed. In these lists you may discover the name of the voter, the year the person registered to vote, address, and occupation.

For Australia, the government database includes Australian Electoral Rolls, listing people eligible to vote, their addresses, and jobs. Canada, too, has many voter lists available online.

The Canadian Jewish Heritage Network website includes immigrant case files, lists of farm settlers, and

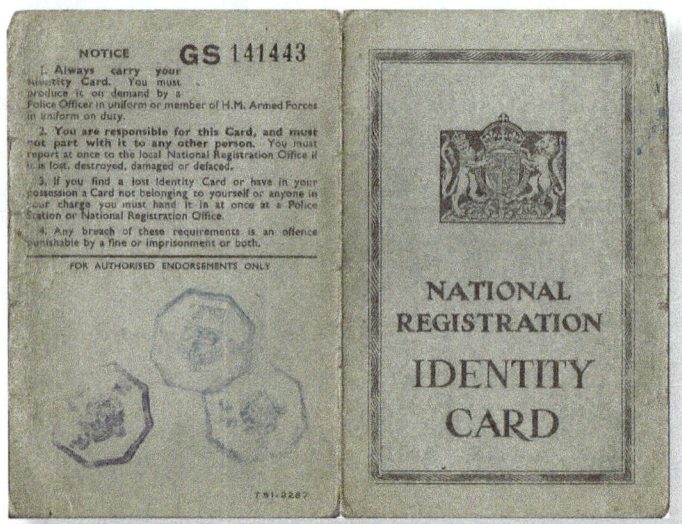

Identity Card used in Britain from 1939–1952: Every British subject was required to carry this at all times; even Jews had their first name listed as their "Christian name" on this card

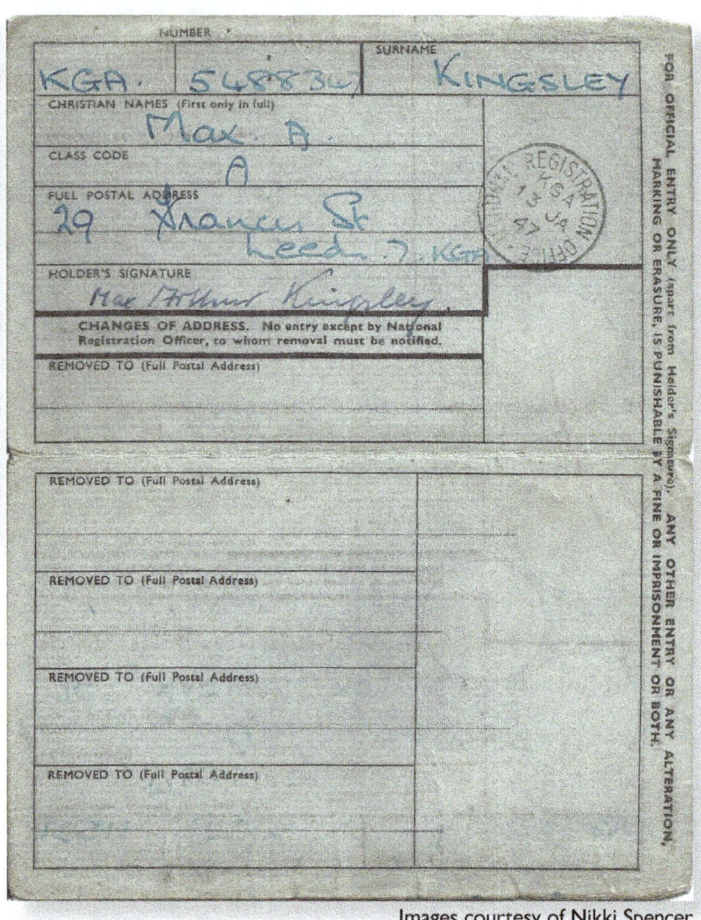

records of a mutual aid society called the Hebrew Sick Benefit Association. This site also has some obituaries from the Yiddish newspaper *Keneder Adler* (Yiddish for "Canadian Eagle"), along with Jewish military deaths.

British telephone books starting from 1880 (the year after public telephone service was introduced to the United Kingdom) are available online through genealogy websites. The British Telecom Archives (digitalarchives.bt.com/Calmview) has a large digital collection of phone books as well. Telephone books also contained advertisements for local businesses, which could be helpful in your search for information about your relatives.

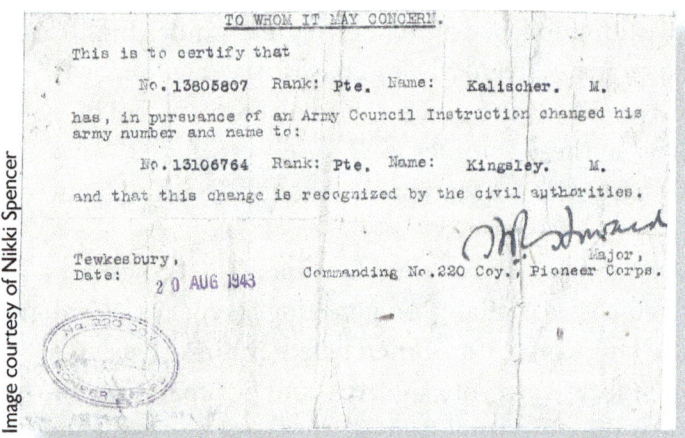

British World War II document describing the change of a Jewish soldier's surname from Kalischer to Kingsley

World War II "dog tag" (military identification) and medals from a British soldier: The word "Jew" was stamped into the tag so authorities would know to handle the body according to Jewish tradition in case the soldier was killed

The United Kingdom also kept city and county directories from the 1600s through the 1900s. The first major county directories were published around 1820.

Along with various forms of city directories, the United Kingdom published commercial directories, which provided alphabetical listings of tradesmen and their addresses. The United Kingdom also published medical registers from 1859 to 1959. These books were published annually and listed the names of all the doctors who were licensed to practice medicine in the United Kingdom and abroad. Who knows? You might discover that one of your ancestors was a doctor in England in the early 1900s!

✡ Continental Europe

Continental Europe, or mainland Europe, has been home to Jews since ancient times. The earliest record of Jews in Europe dates from Greece nearly 2,300 years ago. Soon thereafter, Jews came to live in Roman-ruled Italy. Croatia had a Jewish community 1,800 years ago, and France by the fall of the Roman Empire. Early medieval Jews used the Hebrew word *Ashkenaz* to refer to Germany; *Ashkenazim* eventually came to mean the Jews of central and eastern Europe. Spain was called *Sepharad*, from which the word *Sephardim* is derived. Over time, an incredible variety of customs and traditions has developed among the different Jewish communities of Europe.

Poland, where millions of Jews once lived, was not an independent country during the 1800s, so most pre-World War I Jewish records in what is currently Poland originated in the Austro-Hungarian Empire or Imperial Russia. To find Polish Jewish records, you can search the Polish State Archives at archiwa.gov.pl/en/. The Jewish Records Indexing—Poland (JRI-Poland) organization has undertaken the task of indexing all known Polish Jewish records, and you can search their site at jri-poland.org.

For those with ancestry in the former Austro-Hungarian Empire, which collapsed at the end of World War I, the organization Gesher Galicia (geshergalicia.org) is important for your research. Gesher Galicia collects and indexes Jewish records from the former Empire. Some of the nations that formed after the Empire dissolved include modern Austria, Hungary, Czech Republic, Ukraine, Croatia, and Serbia, plus parts of Italy, Romania, and Poland.

France

Jews have lived in France since the early Middle Ages (5th century–10th century). France currently has the largest Jewish population in Europe, and it has the third largest Jewish population in the world (Israel is number one, and the United States is number two). Today, there are many French Jews who came to France from North Africa and the Mediterranean region.

Many regard King François I's *Ordonnance de Villers-Cotterêts* (Ordinance of Villers-Cotterêts), a major piece of legislation in 1539, as the beginning of systematic civil record-keeping in France, but Jews were generally excluded from these records. In 1802, Emperor Napoleon applied the law equally to all religious groups, including Jews.

Jewish genealogy websites like JewishGen may provide a forum for people doing Jewish genealogical research specifically on France, other French-speaking areas such as Belgium, Luxembourg, and Switzerland,

The *Livret de Famille* ("Family Booklet") is a required document for all French families: It records marriages, births, and deaths

and the former French colonies (e.g., Tunisia and Algeria). These websites provide links to numerous other genealogy resources in both French and English, such as an online 1784 Census of the Jews of Alsace in French, French Postal Codes in English, a Memorial of the Shoah in English, and a France Guide for the Jewish Traveler in English (worldjewishtravel.org).

The *Cercle de Généalogie Juive* (Jewish Genealogy Circle) has a catalogue of its library at genealoj.org/fr. The *Collection de cartes postales historiques de la France* (Collection of historical postcards of France) at ancestry.com is an online database of thousands of historical postcards with photos of different locations in France. This database may be useful for finding photos of places in France where your relatives lived if you don't have any personal photos in your collection.

If you speak French, you can locate the specific *Département* (geographical region or district) in which your French relatives live or lived, search the Internet for that *Département*'s website, and find the *Table décennale* (birth index). Using this index, you can contact the *Département*'s archives to obtain a copy of the desired birth record. For Jewish records before 1802, you can also try contacting the *Consistoire de Paris* through its website (consistoire.org).

Germany

Jews began settling in Germany in medieval times, as they did in France. By 1933, about 522,000 Jews resided in Germany. More than half of the Jewish population left Germany within the first six years of the Nazis coming into power, which occurred in the early 1930s. Some estimate that, by the end of World War II in 1945, about 160,000 to 180,000 German Jews had been killed in the Holocaust.

After the war, Germany's Jewish community began to slowly increase. By the start of the 21st century, Germany had the only expanding Jewish community in Europe. By 2023, the Jewish population of Germany was estimated at 118,000.

The JewishGen German Collection at jewishgen.org combines the information from numerous databases related to Germany. These databases contain entries on Jews who lived in Germany and former German regions like Alsace, Lorraine, Silesia, Posen, and parts of Switzerland and Poland. Additional valuable resources for Germany include Yizkor Books (memorial books documenting Jewish life in towns before and during the Holocaust), a name adoption list index, and a database documenting hundreds of German towns that had Jewish residents prior to World War II.

Ancestry.com has a database called *Sammlung historischer Postkarten aus Deutschland und Österreich* (Collection of Historical Postcards from Germany and Austria) that contains images of thousands of historical postcards with photos from Germany and Austria.

Hungary

The first historical document mentioning Jews in Hungary is from the year 960. By the early 1900s, the Jewish community made up 5% of Hungary's total population, and 23% of the population of Budapest, the capital. During World War II, over 600,000 Jews were killed within Hungary's borders. Today, most

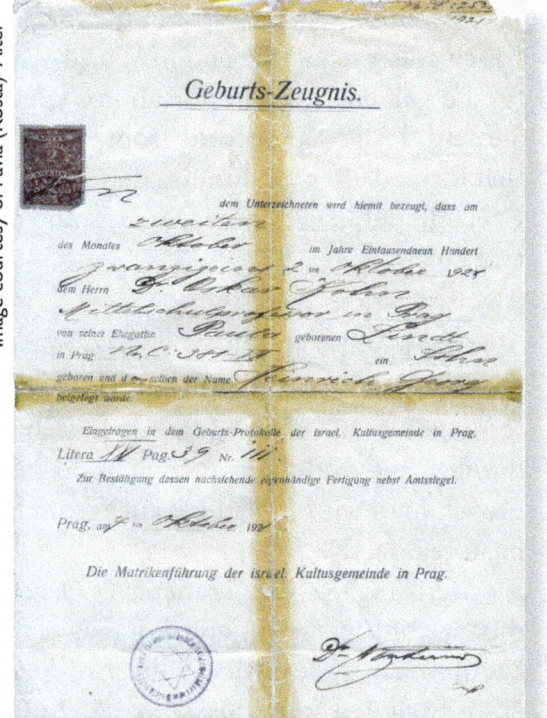

Early 20th-century German language birth record from the Jewish community in Prague, Czechoslovakia (once part of the Austro-Hungarian Empire)

Clues from Beyond the United States 65

of the Jews remaining in Hungary live in Budapest. The Dohány Street Synagogue in Budapest is the largest synagogue in Europe.

The JewishGen Hungary Database at jewishgen.org has information about Jews who resided in the current and former territories of Hungary. This information includes tax and census records, birth and marriage databases, and Yizkor Books.

The National Archives of Hungary has records that can be searched online at mnl.gov.hu; ancestry.com, familysearch.org, and myheritage.com also have microfilmed and digitized records from Hungary.

Ukraine

In Ukraine, the first mention of Jews is in the year 1030. The Soviet Union took over Ukraine in 1922. Before the start of World War II, Jews were the largest national minority group in Ukraine. Between 1941 and 1959, Ukraine's Jewish population decreased almost 70%. Many Jews who had remained in Ukraine by the late 1980s moved to other countries (primarily Israel) in the 1990s during and after the fall of Communism and the breakup of the Soviet Union. Even so, Ukraine still has one of the largest Jewish communities in Europe. Most Jews are in the cities of Kyiv, Dnipro, Kharkiv, and Odesa.

Pages from the 1878 book of Jewish birth records in the city of Zhytomyr, Ukraine, including a record of Stephen Cohen's relatives: The left page is in old Russian, and the right page has the same information in Hebrew (The surnames of the families in Russian are underlined in blue pencil)

Photography by Alexander Krakovsky/CC BY-SA 4.0

The JewishGen Ukraine Database at jewishgen.org contains millions of entries on Jews who lived in the area that is now Ukraine. The entries include Yizkor Books, a Holocaust database, voter lists, business directories, commercial directories, vital records, Russian-Jewish Fallen Soldiers of WWI, and a birth index. You can also find online interactive maps with information about specific provinces, districts, or towns in Ukraine.

Fortunately for present-day genealogy researchers, there is now online access through Alex Krakovsky's wiki site (uk.wikisource.org/wiki/Архів:Єврейське_містечко) to thousands of original Ukrainian Jewish documents and records, especially those from the old Russian Empire. You will need to be able to either read Ukrainian or to translate Ukrainian words in order to understand the website's listings of the record books. When you download the images of the actual documents and records, they will be in the original old Russian and Hebrew handwriting. There are online guides that can help you with deciphering these other languages.

✡ Latin America

The Jews of Latin America have an amazing variety of backgrounds and traditions. Although there are many countries in Latin America with Jewish communities, the countries described below are those that have the largest Jewish populations in Central and South America.

Argentina

Sephardic Jews first settled in Argentina in the early 1500s following the expulsion of Jews from Spain in 1492. Argentina gained its independence from Spain in 1810, and shortly after that, an organized Jewish community began to develop. A Jewish colony was established in Argentina in 1893. Jews from France and other parts of Western Europe also settled in Argentina, and today, the majority of the Jewish population is Ashkenazic. Argentina now has the largest Jewish population in Latin America. Most of Argentina's Jews live in Buenos Aires, Córdoba, and Santa Fe.

There are many search engines, most of which are in Spanish, that can connect you with Argentinian records on topics such as immigration, Jewish colony settlements, Jewish gravesites, and telephone directories.

Search engines include jewishgen.org; cemla.com/buscador, with a database of immigrants to Argentina; and amia.org.ar, an organization of Jews in Argentina. An Argentinian online telephone directory can be found at telexplorer.com.ar.

Brazil

Jews began settling in Brazil after the Inquisition affected Portugal in the 1500s. These early settlers, most of whom were Sephardic, organized the first synagogue in the Americas (Kahal Zur Israel, in Recife) in 1636. Brazil, at this time, was under Dutch rule. Many Moroccan Jews emigrated to Brazil in the 1800s, followed by waves of Polish and Russian Jews escaping pogroms and the Russian Revolution. In the 1930s, Jews fled to Brazil after the Nazis came to power in Europe, and the 1950s saw the arrival of thousands of North African Jews.

You can find information online about Philippson, a Jewish community in Brazil with a fascinating history. Philippson, established in 1904, was the first Jewish colony in Brazil. It consisted of 37 Jewish families (257 people) who emigrated from Bessarabia, an area in what is now the Moldova Republic and parts of Ukraine. The colony was created through the work of the Jewish Colonization Association, an organization established in 1891 by Baron Hirsch to give Jews from Russia and other Eastern European countries the opportunity to farm in colonies that were supported by the Association, especially in Argentina, Brazil, and Canada. The colony was named after Franz Philippson, a Belgian Jewish banker who was the chairman of the Jewish Colonization Association at that time. The 1904 Census List of the original settlers, as well as additional information about the community, is available online at kehilalinks.jewishgen.org. The town, in southern Brazil, is known today as Itaara.

Mexico

Jews began arriving in Mexico in 1519. These initial immigrants were *Marranos* or *Crypto-Jews*, who were forced to convert to Catholicism as a result of the Spanish Inquisition. In the second half of the 19th century, Jews began to emigrate from Europe to Mexico. Jews later arrived from the Ottoman Empire and what is now Syria through the first half of the 20th century.

Today, most of the Jews in Mexico are descended from these immigrants—primarily Yiddish-speaking Ashkenazim or Ladino-speaking Sephardim. JewishGen.com has a Sephardic Special Interest Group that includes information on the Jews of Mexico.

Ancestry.com has databases with census records, birth/marriage/death records, border crossing records, and historical postcards that would be valuable for any research you do on the Jews in Mexico. Jeff Malka's sephardicgen.com and myheritage.com also have detailed information on the Jews of Mexico.

If you have relatives from the countries mentioned in this chapter, list them, and their town and country:

Person	Town	Country

Across the Ocean: Your Own Voyage of Discovery

Almost everyone in North America—most likely you as well—has at least one ancestor who came from a different continent. Part of your voyage of discovery about your family therefore involves finding out how, when, and where your ancestors travelled.

✡ Arriving in "The Golden Land"

Eastern European Jews often called America "*Di Goldeneh Medineh*," which is Yiddish for "The Golden Land." If your ancestors came here before World War II, which started in 1939, they most likely had to cross an ocean. Flying, driving, or walking here was not an option, so your ancestors had to come by boat. In the late 1800s and early 1900s, there were a number of commercial steamship companies that regularly sailed across the Atlantic Ocean between Europe and North America, taking millions of immigrants to the New World.

The most famous port of entry into North America was Ellis Island, in New York Harbor, but there were many other places where people arrived. For example, many people entered the United States through Boston, Philadelphia, Baltimore, San Francisco, New Orleans, and Galveston. They also might have sailed into Halifax, Canada. Sometimes people traveled first to Canada or Mexico, and then crossed the border into the United States: In the 1920s, they might have traveled by boat from Windsor, Ontario to Detroit, or taken the Grand Trunk Railway from Montréal to New York.

Geography whiz alert!

✡ Leaving the "Old Country"

From which ports did your ancestors leave? The major emigration ports in Europe included Amsterdam and Rotterdam (Netherlands); Antwerp (Belgium); Bremen and Hamburg (Germany); Cherbourg and Le Havre (France); Hull, Liverpool, and Southampton (England); Trieste, Palermo, Naples, and Genoa (Italy); and Liepāja, also called Libau (Latvia).

In nearly all these cases, emigrants had records documenting their journey. When travelers bought tickets and boarded a steamship, the ship's crew compiled a list of all the people on board. This list was called a *ship manifest*. At the end of these overseas journeys, the manifests were delivered to the Customs Office in the American port and filed. Many years later, these files were photographed and copied onto film using a process called *microfilming*. You are lucky because, with the invention of the Internet, most of these microfilmed ship manifests have been scanned and posted on websites

Some major ports of departure for Jews

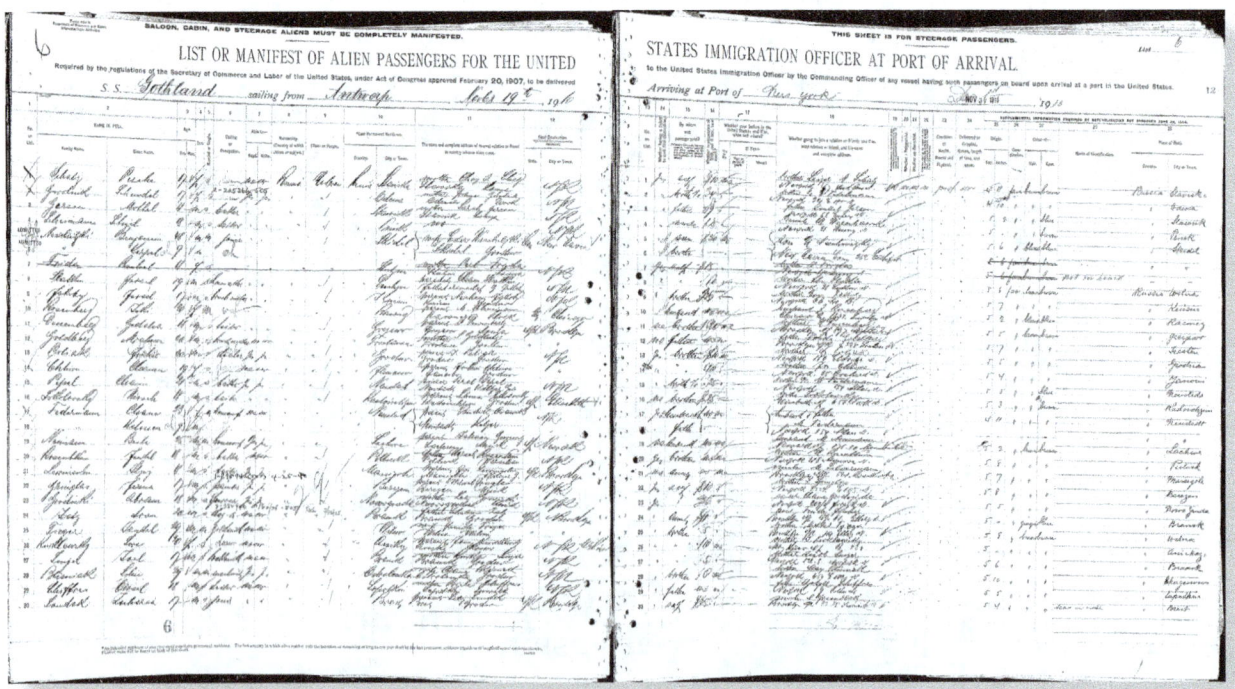

Manifest of ship arriving from Antwerp, Belgium in late 1910: You will see names, addresses, ages, professions, and other important details about the passengers, including a relative of Stephen Cohen

Receipt that Caryn Alter's relative got for a visa to come to the USA

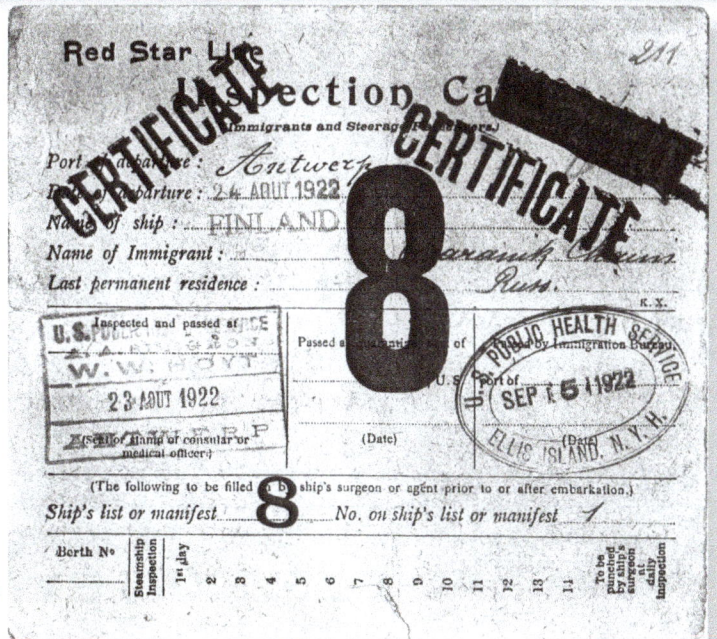

Ship ticket for Caryn Alter's relative's travel to the USA

like ancestry.com, familysearch.org, myheritage.com, and statueofliberty.org. The search engine stevemorse.org accesses and organizes immigration information from other databases.

Records were also kept at many ports of departure, but most of these records appear to have been destroyed. One exception is the Hamburg port: Most of its departure lists still exist, and are available online through ancestry.com.

★ So How Do I Find These Records?

WORK BACKWARDS IN TIME

If your family already knows the name of your relatives' ship, try to find the ship manifest that was presented to the Customs Office when your ancestors arrived in the United States. If you don't know the name of the ship, you can find that information on the Internet.

There are several search engines and websites with databases that contain documents related to Jewish emigration—especially to the United States through Ellis Island. For example, you can try ancestry.com, familysearch.org, myheritage.com, and statueofliberty.org.

★ Myth-Busting Alert!! Myth-Busting Alert!!

Maybe you have heard stories about how your last name was "changed at Ellis Island." It's not true. It's what we call in Yiddish a "*bobeh-mayseh*" (a fable or fairy-tale).

NOBODY'S NAME WAS CHANGED AT ELLIS ISLAND

Think about it. Ellis Island processed thousands upon thousands of people every month for entry into the United States. There certainly wasn't enough time for an immigration clerk to ask a traveler's name several times, and then either intentionally or unintentionally write down the incorrect name in English—especially with long lines of people waiting!

Contrary to popular belief, this name-changing never happened, and there are no books or official lists containing names altered at Ellis Island. The clerks examined the ship manifest from the port of departure, and compared the names on that list to the names of people entering the port in their new country. If people changed their names, it happened:

1. **Before they got on the ship, before the ship manifest was written (or typed, in later years), or perhaps even before they received tickets or a visa to leave their home country:** Maybe your ancestor bought a ticket under a false name. Or maybe your male relative changed his name to escape the Russian military draft.
2. **After they left Ellis Island:** In those days there were no computers to keep track of people, and no social media accounts to prove your identity. Once you left the island for New York City or New Jersey, you could call yourself whatever you wanted, as long as you weren't deceiving people. You were free to choose an "American-sounding" name after you left the port of arrival in the United States.

So…no clerk ever changed anyone's name at Ellis Island. The United States Citizenship and Immigration Services (USCIS) even conducted its own historical studies, and found no truth to this myth, however amusing it may be.

Aunt Linda and Grandpa Mark might have some colorful stories about name changes, and the reasons for them. But now you know names weren't altered by an immigration officer at Ellis Island!

✦ Schwartz or Szwarc? A Spelling Lesson

When you search for a ship manifest, this is Golden Rule #1:

BE FLEXIBLE WITH SPELLING

Why?

The English language uses the letters of the Roman alphabet (A, B, C). If your ancestors came from a country that did not use the Roman alphabet, they wrote their names using a different alphabet, such as Cyrillic (А, Б, В, Г), used in the Russian Empire. The ship manifests, however, had to be in English if the ship was sailing to the United States or Canada. Therefore, the passengers' names were written down by emigration officials at the port of departure the way they looked or sounded in their original language, but by using letters from the English language.

Different emigration officials could choose to spell the same name many different ways. For example, let's look at the last name "Schwartz." In German it might be spelled "Schwarz." In Polish it might be spelled "Szwarc" or "Szwarz." All the spellings are different, but for a name with the exact same pronunciation!

In fact, not only did emigration officials spell the same surname (last name) in different ways, but so might local officials writing civil records entries and even the immigrants themselves (if they could write their names). William Shakespeare was known to have signed his name as "Shakspere," "Shakspēr," and "Shakspeare!"

It's important to remember that when your great-great-grandfather was growing up in Russia, his name wasn't Bernie or Sol. Those were likely names "adopted" after arriving in an English-speaking country. In Russia and other parts of Eastern Europe, Jews generally used only their Jewish (Hebrew or Yiddish) names, although some Jews also had a secular (non-religious) name that was used in business or socially. To track down your ancestors, you will therefore have to find out their Jewish names, or possibly take a good guess. Maybe Bernie was "Baruch" or, more likely in Eastern Europe, "Boruch." Maybe Sol was "Shlomo," but more likely in Eastern Europe, "Shloymeh" or "Shleymeh."

What does your last name mean? From what language is your last name derived? Was it changed upon immigration? If so, what was it in the "Old Country?"

Your last name	
Original last name in the "Old Country," if it was changed later	
Language from which your last name is derived	
Meaning of your last name (if known)	
If your last name was originally written in another alphabet, write it in that alphabet (if you can)	

✶ A Name Puzzle

One of the authors, Stephen Cohen, had a great-great aunt, "Tanteh Beckie Newman." *Tanteh* is one word for "aunt" in Yiddish (the other is *moomeh* or *meemeh*, depending on the dialect). Tanteh Beckie wasn't called Beckie Newman in Belarus (now an independent country, but part of the Russian Empire when she was born there). Here's the puzzle: What WAS she called?

She was the younger sister of Stephen's great-grandmother, who was born around 1883, so we can guess that Beckie was born about 1885. She came to the United States just before Stephen's great-grandmother (who arrived in 1911), but after Stephen's great-grandfather and his brother (who arrived in 1907 and worked in the United States to earn money for tickets for the rest of the family). So we know she arrived sometime between 1907 and 1911. From family stories, we also know she was from the town of Lakhva in Belarus.

The challenge, then, is to find a Beckie Newman (who was not called Beckie Newman at that time) who was in her twenties and arrived in New York between 1907 and 1911.

One of Stephen's cousins was named after Tanteh Beckie, so we know that Beckie's Hebrew name was Beyleh (as discussed in the chapter on cemeteries). We can now search for a *Beyleh Newman* using Steve Morse's Ellis Island search engine (stevemorse.org), one of the resources available for immigration records:

Tanteh Beckie Newman in the Catskill Mountains, New York, 1920s

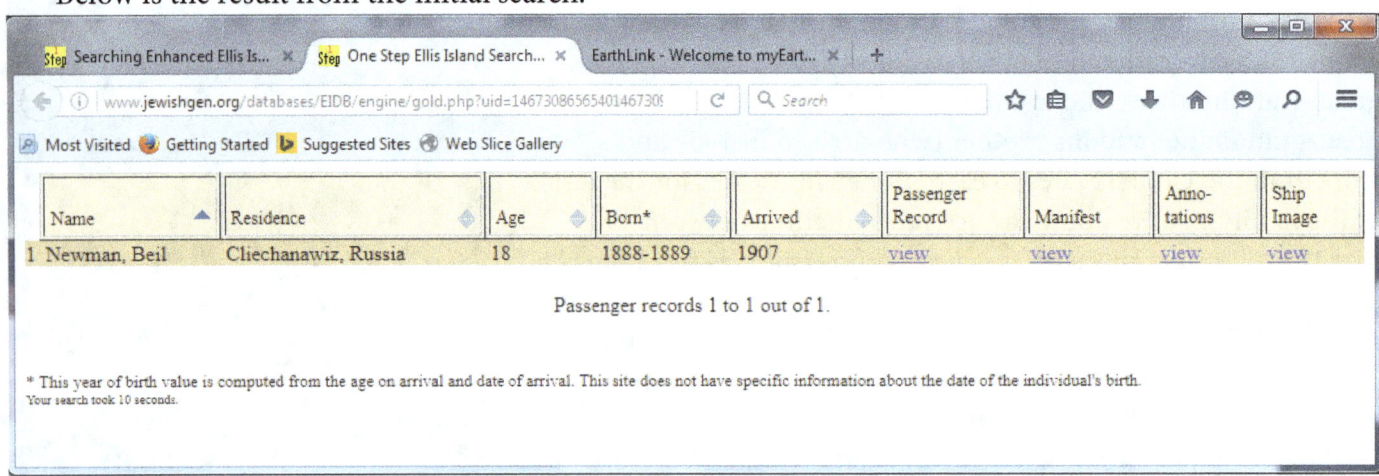

Click "sounds like" so you'll see names with slightly different spellings.

Give yourself a range of years, so you have a better chance of finding the person.

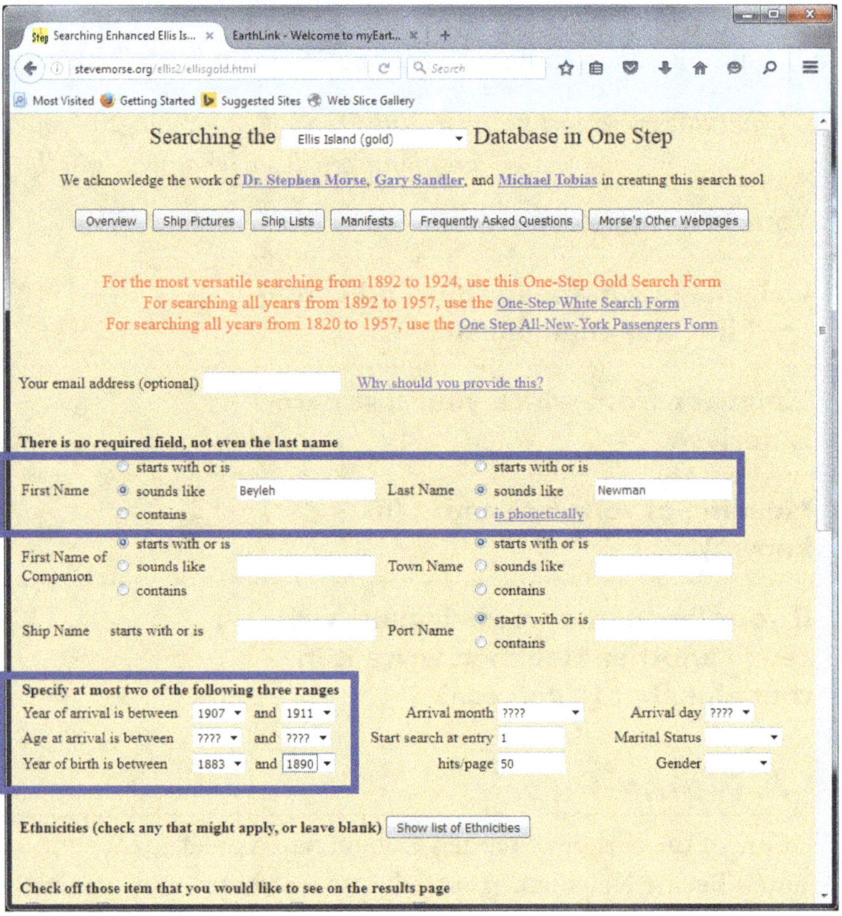

Below is the result from the initial search:

Name	Residence	Age	Born*	Arrived	Passenger Record	Manifest	Annotations	Ship Image
1 Newman, Beil	Cliechanawiz, Russia	18	1888-1889	1907	view	view	view	view

Passenger records 1 to 1 out of 1.

* This year of birth value is computed from the age on arrival and date of arrival. This site does not have specific information about the date of the individual's birth.
Your search took 10 seconds.

Unfortunately, this isn't the right woman: Beyleh wasn't from Cliechanawiz. This might mean that her last name WASN'T Newman, which is an English surname. In Yiddish, it could have been Nayman (which means "new man"). So let's try *Beyleh Nayman*:

Across the Ocean: Your Own Voyage of Discovery   75

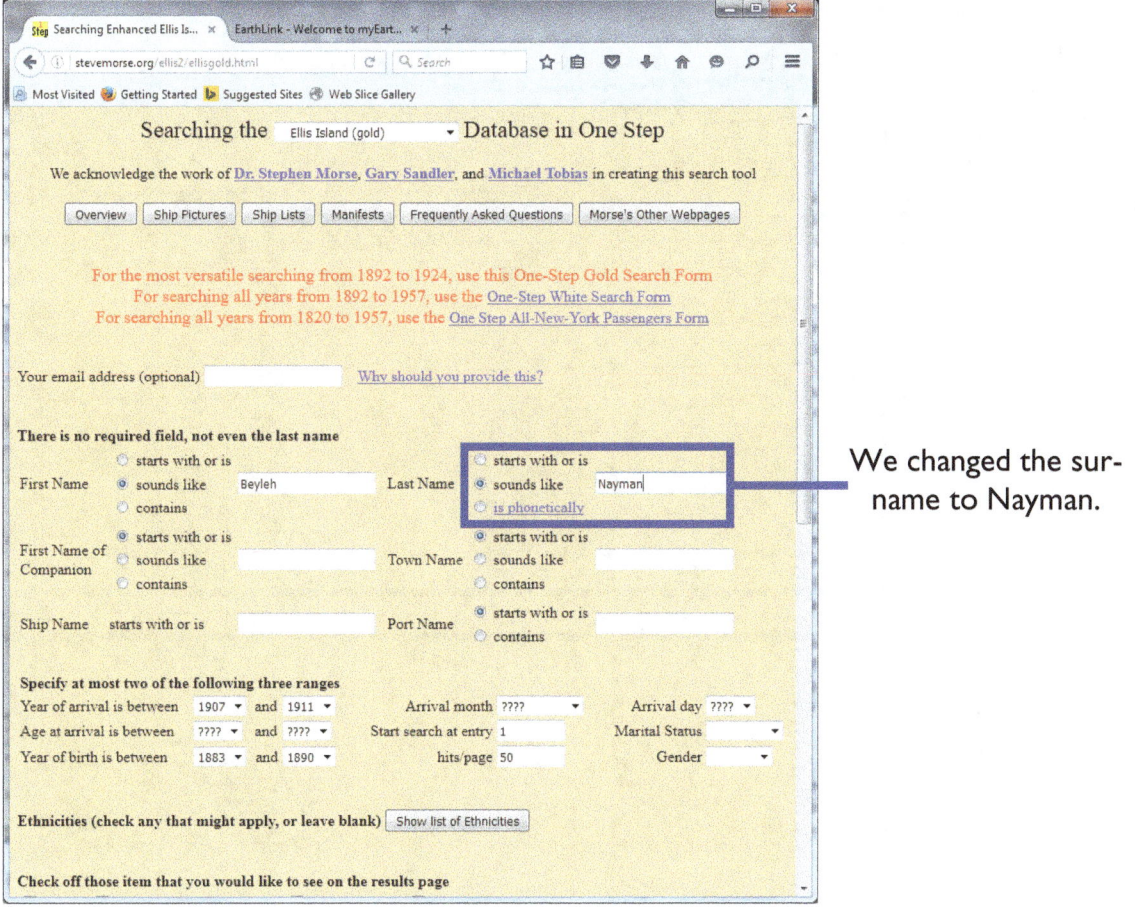

We changed the surname to Nayman.

The result of that search is below.

Look at #12 on the list: Beile Neimann from Sachwe, Russia, who was born around 1884–1885 and came to the United States in 1910. This is the same information listed on the manifest shown at the beginning of this chapter. However, the town name "Sachwe" seems odd.

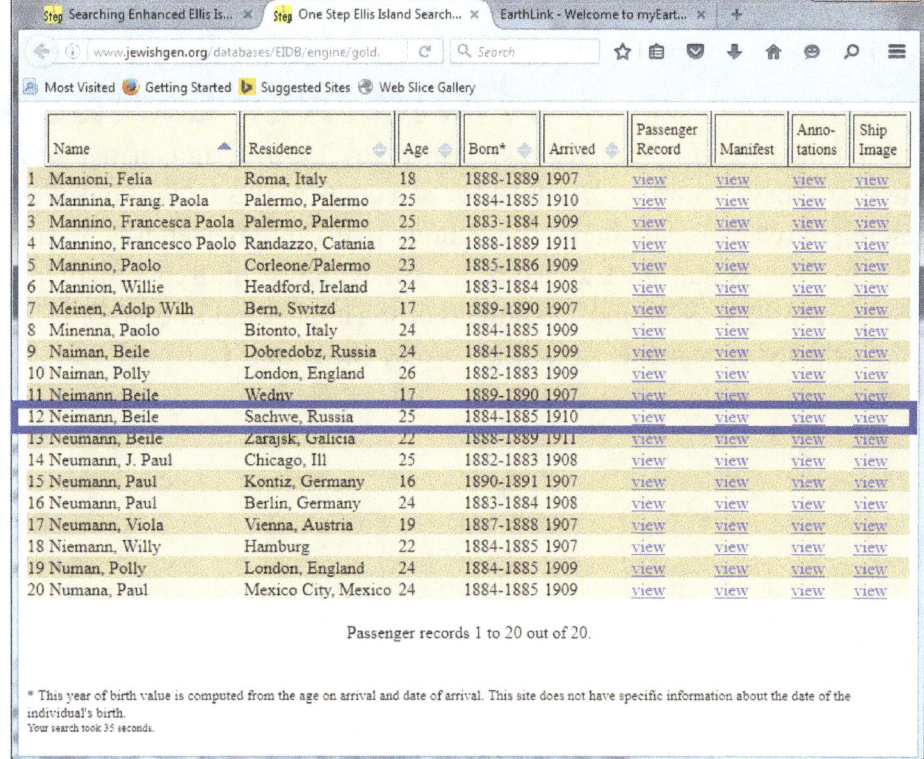

Let's take a closer look at the first page of the actual manifest on the next page:

Look at line #19 carefully (we outlined it for you). The town name (right part of Column 10) listed in the Ellis Island database (statueofliberty.org) as "Sachwe" might actually start with a curly "L" and be spelled "Lachwe."

Ellis Island ship manifest from 1910: Line 19 is Beile Neimann

Now we will follow Golden Rule #2:

PRETEND YOU ARE READING IN ANOTHER LANGUAGE

In our search for Tanteh Beckie Newman, "Lachwe" in German or Polish would be read as "Lakhva." Hence we have found our relative! We can confirm this by looking at more of the manifest close up. From talking to relatives, Stephen Cohen knows that Tante Beyleh was married, but never had children. The manifest shows that she traveled by herself, with no children—further evidence that this might be the correct person. Also, Column 11 shows that she left behind in the "Old Country" her father, "Zalman Gurevitz," whose first name is already known by the author (see page 52).

Across the Ocean: Your Own Voyage of Discovery   77

Try using the tips in this chapter to discover information about one of your relatives. Then fill in the following table using Stephen Cohen's information on the left as an example. You may have to leave some details blank if you don't know them:

	Author's information about a great-great-aunt	Information about one of your relatives
Relative's name after emigration	Beckie Newman	
Jewish (Yiddish or Hebrew) first name (all possible spellings)	Beyleh, Beile	
All possible spellings of original last name	Nayman, Naiman, Neiman, Neimann	
Country of birth	Belarus (but part of Russian Empire back then)	
Town of birth (all possible spellings)	Sachwe, Lachwe, Lakhva	
Date of birth	1885	
Estimated year of arrival	1907–1911	
Actual year of arrival	1910	
Port of departure	Antwerp, Belgium	
Port of arrival	Ellis Island, United States	
Name of ship	Gothic	

✡ Other Emigration Records

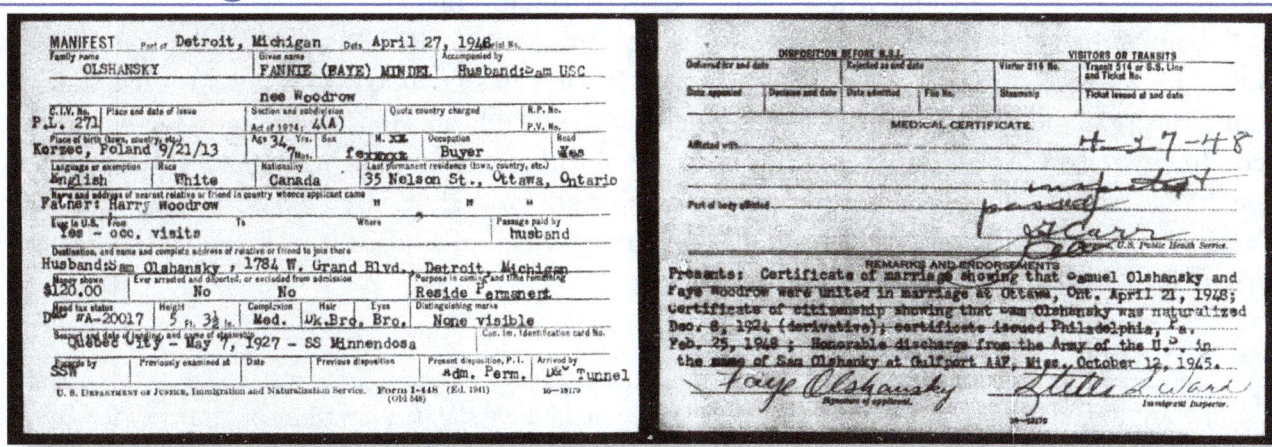

Border-crossing record from Detroit, Michigan, 1948

This Detroit border-crossing record is for a relative of Stephen Cohen. The person left Windsor, Ontario in Canada, and crossed the border into Detroit, Michigan in the USA. The front of the card (left side of the image) shows the date of crossing, name and address, and even the name of the ship (the S.S. *Minnendosa*) on which the relative arrived in Québec City, Canada in 1927. Note the signature on the back of the card (bottom left corner of the image on page 77) of the relative who crossed the border.

If your relatives were lucky enough to travel overseas by airplane, even for a business trip, in the 1940s or 1950s, you can find an airplane manifest for that trip at ancestry.com.

On the right is a manifest for Stephen Cohen's relatives who returned to New York City from Bermuda on Pan American World Airways in 1955.

If your relatives traveled here across the ocean by ship, you can likely find a photograph of the actual ship by searching a website that includes immigration records.

Passenger manifest from Idlewild Airport (now JFK Airport) in New York City, 1955

✦ Detention of Immigrants

No, we're not talking about being sent to the principal's office at school! Rather, we mean that sometimes immigrants were detained, or held, at ports of arrival because of medical problems or other reasons. The United States (as well as other countries) did not want people who carried deadly diseases to enter the country, nor people who were unable to support themselves financially.

At the top of the next page is an example of a list of immigrants (called "aliens") detained at Ellis Island. Of course, an "*alien*" is not someone from outer space. It refers to someone who is not a United States citizen. Line 10 shows the name of a relative of Stephen Cohen. It indicates that this relative is a mother with four children who had to wait until the father, who was already living in the United States, could retrieve them at 2:37 PM on July 29, 1914 after they ate five meals (one for each family member).

Caryn Alter's grandfather was detained on Ellis Island because of a possible problem with his eyes. He was eventually allowed to enter the United States.

✦ Passports

If you want to travel to another country, you usually need a *passport*, a small booklet provided by your government identifying you as a citizen of that land, and asking that you be given legal protection while visiting another country. Many people were required to obtain passports from their country's government in order to leave their home in the late 1800s, although at that time passports were not required by the United States for entry.

For people with little money, collecting the funds to buy a passport was not easy. Additionally, male

Part of an Ellis Island ship manifest from 1914 showing people held temporarily at the island: The name of a relative of Stephen Cohen is outlined

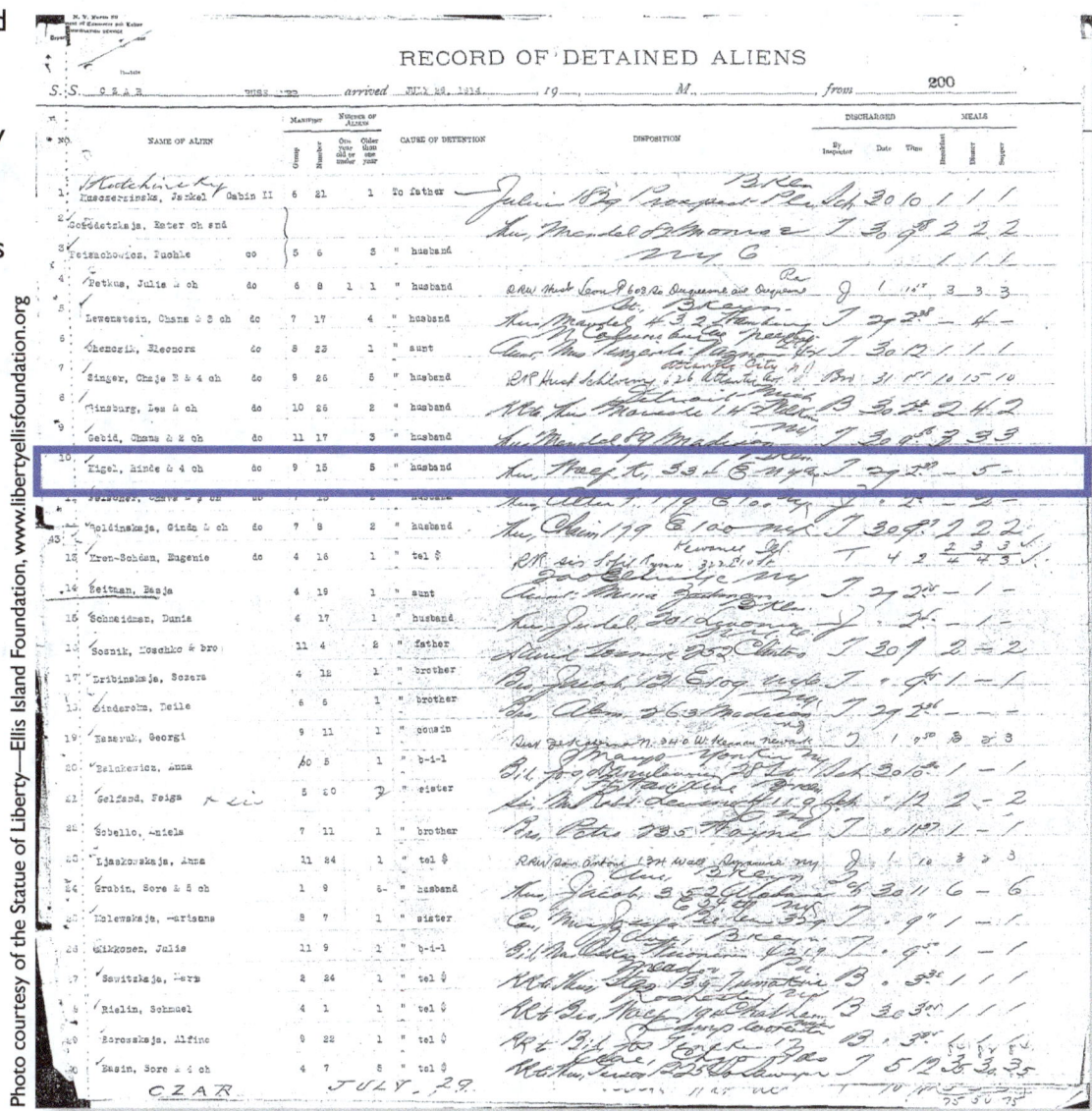

Photo courtesy of the Statue of Liberty—Ellis Island Foundation, www.libertyellisfoundation.org

Jews in Russia in the late 1800s had to prove that they had served their required time in the military. Jewish men often tried to avoid military service because of poor living conditions, anti-Semitism, and non-kosher food. They sometimes had to bribe or pay people extra money to get a passport, or they obtained a fake passport (and thereby assumed a new identity).

Passports can be valuable sources of genealogical information. On the next page is an example from Stephen Cohen's collection. The title page of a passport from the Russian Empire of a century ago is shown on the top left of the next page. If you've studied some German or French in school, you may be able to translate *Unterschrift des Inhabers* or *Signature du porteur* (near the bottom of the cover) as "Signature of the bearer." The great-grandmother of the author signed her own name as "*Perla Naiman*" in Russian script on the cover. (In America she was known as "Pearl Newman," another example of name-changing!)

On the right is the inside of the passport. It is written entirely in Russian. The left page gives the names and ages of the passport holder and her children: Perla Zalmanova Naiman (age 30), Sheyndla (age 9), Dina (age 7), Dovid-Meyer (age 5), and Daniel (age 4). The right page shows the city (Minsk) where the passport was obtained, and the year it was issued (October 18, 1911). Around the border in German and French you can see *Reise Pass* ("passport") and *Passeport pour l'étranger* ("foreign passport").

Russian passport of Perla Naiman showing her signature written in Russian

Interior of passport

Names and ages of Perla Naiman and her children

Place (Minsk) and date of passport (October 18, 1911)

By the way, the middle name "Zalmanova" means "daughter of Zalman" in Russian, which conveniently provides you with the name of Perla's father!

This is a good example of why it can be exciting and rewarding to learn the alphabets of other languages—it can help you enormously with your genealogical research.

The "Old Country"

OFTEN IMMIGRANTS TO A NEW COUNTRY will call the country of their birth the "Old Country." They may have some fond memories of the "Old Country," but some of the memories may be painful or unpleasant, depending on the immigrant's experiences there.

✡ *Where Jews Lived in Eastern Europe*

Before World War I, which ended in 1918 and disrupted many borders, countries, and empires, most Ashkenazic Jews lived in either the Russian Empire or Austria-Hungary. The country of Poland didn't exist in the 19th century, so sometimes you may hear of (or see in documents) the term "Russian Poland," because the Russian Empire governed provinces that were once (and now again are) part of independent Poland.

In the Russian Empire, Jews were only allowed to live in a particular geographical area at the western border of Russia. This area where Jews were allowed to live was called the *Pale of Settlement*. The Jews in the Pale of Settlement made up between 5% and 15% of the total population, but this percentage was often much higher in major cities. If your family came from Russia, they most likely lived in the Pale of Settlement.

Eastern Europe before World War I (1914): The Russian Empire is red, with its Pale of Settlement in pink and divided into gubernias, or provinces (some major towns and cities are marked)

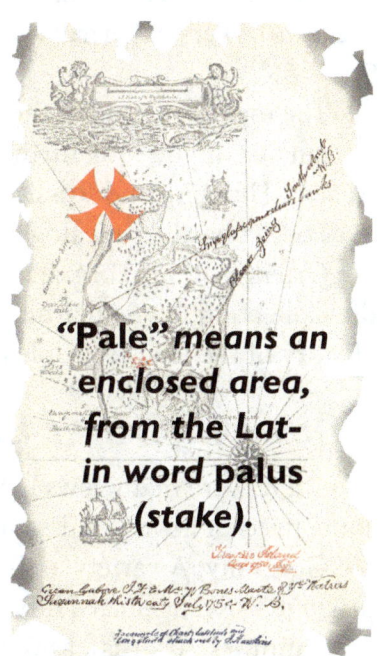

"Pale" means an enclosed area, from the Latin word *palus* (stake).

You may hear that a relative came from "Voliner Gubernia" or "Minsker Gubernia." The Pale of Settlement was divided into *gubernias* (provinces), each named for an important town in that gubernia. So a person from Kovno Gubernia was not necessarily from the city of Kovno, but lived in that province. This is similar to someone saying, "I'm not from New York City, but I do live in New York State in the city of Albany."

100-ruble banknote from the Russian Empire

Many Jews came from Austria-Hungary, an empire which broke up after World War I into the separate countries of Austria and Hungary. Some important Austro-Hungarian cities with Jewish populations in the 19th century include Lemberg, Budapest, Kraków, Czernowitz, and Brody. Southern parts of what is now Poland were ruled by the Austro-Hungarian Empire.

The era from World War I to World War II was extremely disruptive for people who lived in Central and Eastern Europe. Borders changed and nationalities shifted. There were many immigrants who, when filling out United States naturalization papers or census records, claimed Russian nationality on one document and Polish nationality on another.

These changes in Europe brought challenges to the Jews living there. The American Jewish Joint Distribution Committee (known as "The Joint"), formed in 1914, provided aid and relief for Jews of the "Old Country." Many of its archived records and indexes are now available at archives.jdc.org, and include names and case files from World Wars I and II.

✡ Where Jews Lived in the Mediterranean Basin

Around the eastern end of the Mediterranean Sea was the Ottoman Empire, which collapsed during World War I. The Ottoman Empire was welcoming to Jews in the Middle Ages, so when Spain and Portugal expelled Jews in the 1490s, many of these Jews (called *Sephardim*) settled in the Ottoman Empire. There were already other communities of Jews in that area, notably the Romaniote (Greek) Jews and, farther east, the Jews of Persia. Perhaps your family has ancestors who came from the lands around the Mediterranean Sea.

The map at the top of the next page shows some major Sephardic communities around the Mediterranean Sea. If you look further north, there is some overlap with the *Ashkenazic* Jewish communities of Austria-Hungary and Russia.

For Sephardic genealogy research, explore the website for *Les Fleurs de l'Orient* (French for "Flowers of the Orient") at farhi.org. It concentrates on Sephardim from the Ottoman Empire. The Jeff Malka Sephardic Collection is a Sephardic online database available through jewishgen.org. The Central Archives for the History of the Jewish People in Jerusalem (nli.org.il/en) has some documents related to Jews from Greece.

✡ Jews in Other Lands

There were many Jews living in other parts of Europe in the 19th century. Some lived in large cities, some lived in towns, and some lived in small rural villages or *shtetls*.

Germany: A variety of German Jewish records can be found online at ancestry.com, even from—surprisingly—Evangelical-Lutheran Parish records (Jews were often haphazardly included in other religious communities' records), as well as Hesse-Nassau Civil Records and Church Books. The German Collection

Some Sephardic communities bordering the Mediterranean Sea

at jewishgen.org includes the 1933 German Towns Project, a list of Jewish inhabitants of German communities as of 1933 and, if known, their fate. Other websites to try include familysearch.org and myheritage.com. The Center for Jewish History (cjh.org) has a Jewish Family History Research Guide for Germany.

Italy: There is extensive information at jewishgen.org about the Jewish communities in Italy. The *Centro di Documentazione Ebraica Contemporanea* (Center of Contemporary Jewish Documentation), at cdec.it, and the italian-family-history.com/jewish/genealogy.html website, have archives related to Jews in Italy.

Other Countries: Several isolated Jewish communities around the world include the Beta Israel Jews of Ethiopia, and the Bene Israel and Cochin Jews of India. Indeed, Jews have lived on nearly every continent and in nearly every country during recorded history.

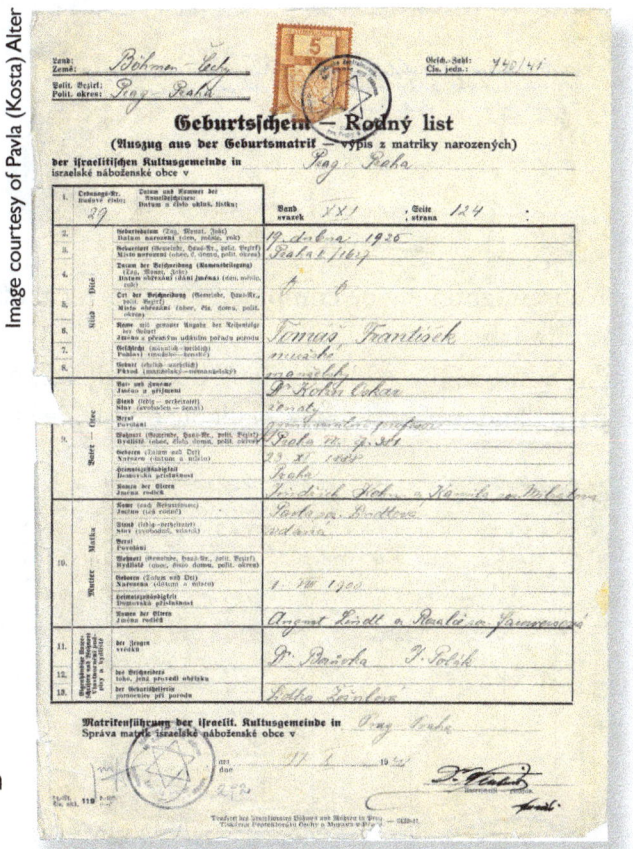

1941 dual-language (German and Czech) birth record from the Jewish community in Prague

✶ Kahal Records and Civil Records

Kahal is the Hebrew word for the Jewish community in a town. Many Jewish communities in Europe kept track of births, *brit milah* ("covenant of circumcision" ceremonies), marriages, divorces, and deaths, usually because the local government required them to do so. Depending upon the country in which your ancestors lived, you may be able to find such records.

This is where your alphabet and language skills will come in handy: These records are likely to be in

84   The "Old Country"

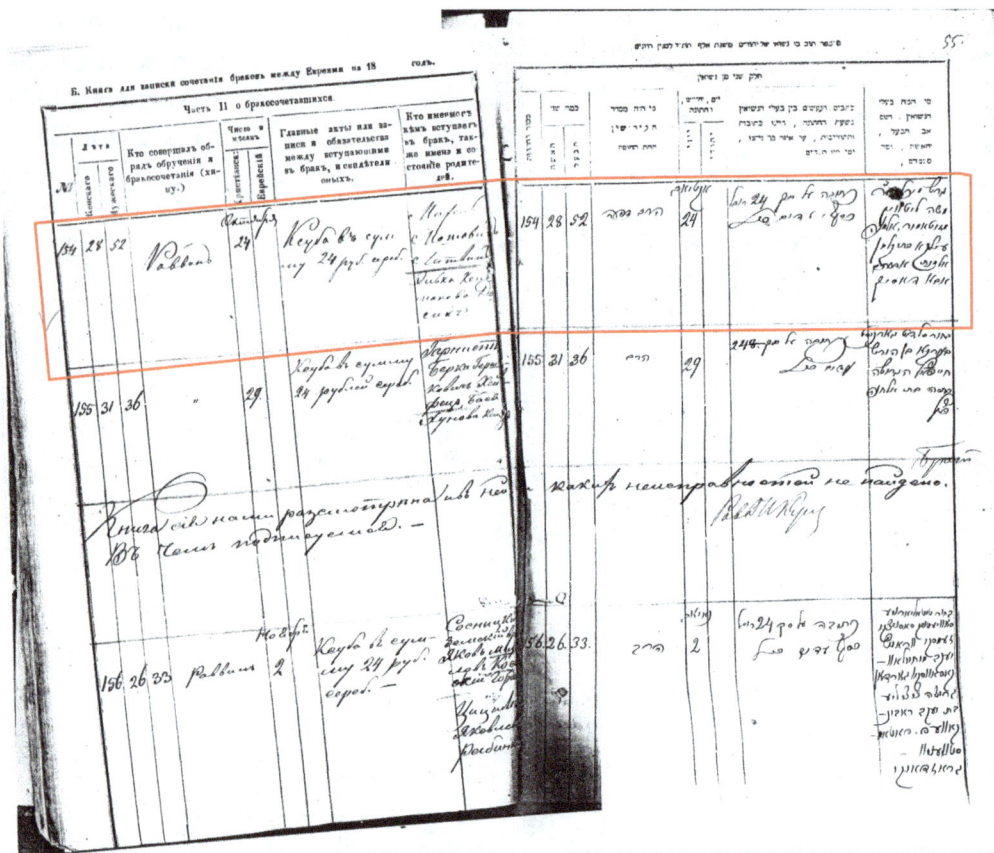

Pages from the 1869 book of marriage records from the *kahal* (Jewish community) of Zhytomyr, Ukraine. The left side is written in Russian, and the right side is in Hebrew. A marriage of Stephen Cohen's great-great-great aunt is outlined in red.

Hebrew, and may be combined with the local official language, such as Polish, Russian, German, Hungarian or French.

Some of these records have been indexed, or sorted, by various organizations like geshergalicia.org and jri-poland.org, and made available online. Jewishgen.org has Special Interest Groups (SIGs) that are devoted

Pages from the 1901 book of marriage records from the *kahal* of Lakhva, Belarus. Like the Ukrainian document above, the left side is written in Russian, and the right side is in Hebrew. The marriage of Stephen Cohen's great-grandparents is outlined in red. You can see the difference in handwriting between this and the Ukrainian record.

to specific geographic areas like Lithuania, Germany, and Hungary, or certain gubernias in Russia such as Suwalk or Grodno. There are genealogy websites dedicated specifically to Sephardic Jews (Jeff Malka's sephardicgen.com) and Iraqi Jews (ijarchive.org). Usually each SIG hosts its own web page. JewishGen has an online index of the SIGs' records. If your family is related to famous rabbis, there is even a Rabbinic SIG called Rav-SIG at JewishGen to help you with your search. Indexing such records requires a lot of work, so some of these SIGs charge a membership fee to help pay for researchers to visit archives, photocopy records, and translate the key bits of information.

The Polish State Archives (an *archive* is a place that stores public records or historical materials), at archiwa.gov.pl, has made available many of its records. Jewish Records Indexing–Poland (JRI–Poland for short), which launched in 1995, has assembled an index of millions of vital records (e.g., births, deaths, marriages) from Polish towns. They are now available on its website (jri-poland.org), and new records are continually being added.

The Routes to Roots Foundation website at rtrfoundation.org has a searchable database of archives from the former Pale of Settlement.

So when you hear Aunt Lilly and Uncle Joe tell you that there is nothing left of their grandparents' childhood town because it was destroyed during World War II, all is not lost: Even though many of the town's buildings may have been destroyed, its stories and records may have survived. You will see, as you read this book, that there are researchers hard at work examining crumbling record books in many of these towns, and preserving this information for future generations of genealogists. Yes, some records were destroyed during wars, but lots of valuable records remain!

✡ Census Records in the "Old Country"

The Russian Empire conducted occasional censuses starting in 1795, and some of these records still exist. Because the Russian Empire collapsed in 1917, and borders of the new countries changed throughout the 20th century, the challenge is figuring out which governmental archives hold the census books you need for your research. On the next page is a record (outlined) of Stephen Cohen's great-great-grandfather (age 17½), and this relative's sister, niece, and mother, from the All-Russia Census of 1858, which he obtained by contacting the Zhytomyr State Archives in Ukraine.

Austria-Hungary conducted censuses in 1828 and 1869, plus a census of Jews (called the *Conscriptio Judæorum* in Latin) in 1848.

A number of local towns in Austria-Hungary also ran censuses (both general and for Jews alone) in the late 18th and early 19th centuries. Often the Jewish censuses were designed to impose special taxes (so-called *Tolerance Taxes*—more on taxes later in this chapter) on Jews living in that area.

The "Old Country"

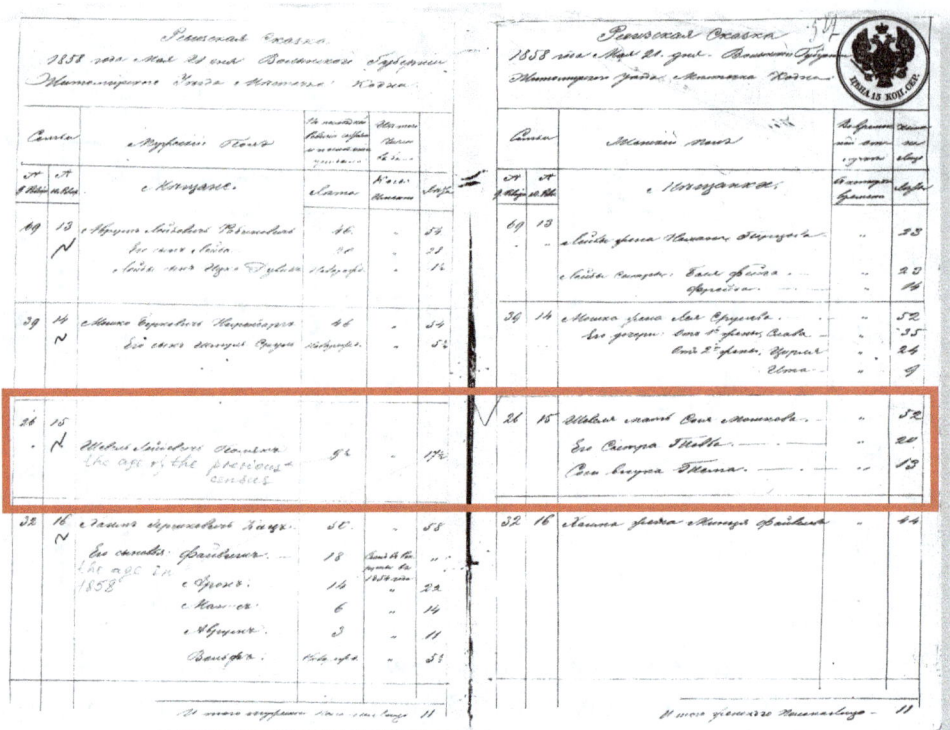

1858 All-Russia Census Record from Kodnya (now in Ukraine), showing Stephen Cohen's great-great-grandfather and relatives

✦ Telephone Books

As telephones became popular around the world in the 1920s and 1930s, *telephone books* began to be printed. Telephone books generally have the name of people or businesses, plus their addresses. Remember that telephones were a luxury in many parts of the world until well after World War II, so not everyone had telephones.

The United States Library of Congress began systematically collecting residential and organizational telephone books from many countries in 1937, and has posted this information online at loc.gov/rr/european/tel.html. Many Jews lived in the Borough of Brooklyn in New York City during the 20th century. You can look up your family members if they had a telephone number in Brooklyn using the Brooklyn Public Library's set of digitized old telephone books. These are available through the webpage of the Internet Archive (archive.org), a digital library of free books and other materials.

✦ Business Directories

Nowadays, if you need to get the phone number of your local computer store or restaurant, it's as easy as a few clicks on a keyboard. But before telephones could be found in every home and shop, it used to be commonplace—including in Poland and Russia—to print directories of local businesses.

There are Polish Business Directories available for certain years from the 1920s and 1930s online. There are also business directories from Russia from the 1890s and 1900s available online. These directories may include name, patronymic (name derived from the name of a father or male ancestor), town, and occupation/job, and may also include the address.

Other examples of directories you can find online are the 1891 Industry and Trade Directory of Hungary and the 1925 Carpathian Ruthenia Business Directory. Many of these directories from the "Old Country" can be found at ancestry.com, familysearch.org, jewishgen.org, and jri-poland.org.

✦ Tax and Voter Records

Throughout history, the citizens of different countries and regions have paid taxes, or fees, to the government. The government uses this tax money to run the country and to provide services for its citizens.

Some of these tax records still exist, and can provide helpful clues regarding your relatives. These tax records usually provide the first names and last names of all the community's heads of household. (In those

Find the clues to the envelope's origin: The stamps say "CCCP" (Russian for "USSR"), and the postmark is from Kaunas, now in Lithuania

days, the head of the household was usually a man.) These records might also list the wife's name, number of family members, job or occupation, financial status or social class, age, and date of death.

In the modern world, "class" has no legal meaning. But centuries ago in Europe and Asia, *social class* referred to whether a person was a peasant, merchant, trader, or member of the nobility. Jews were often considered a unique class, because they didn't practice the government's official religion. Sometimes Jews were even considered the king's or emperor's personal property to do with as he wished.

The 1846 Tax and Voters Lists for Lithuania record the head of household's and wife's names. Lithuania's lists from 1892 provide the taxpayer's profession and the number of males in the household.

The information in these Lithuanian tax records came from:

- Real estate records (records relating to owning a home)
- Lists of farmers, estate holders, and people who lived in apartment buildings
- Lists of donations to charity and financial aid to the poor
- Inheritance and other legal records

In Lithuanian communities, records were kept for different types of taxes, including local and state taxes, real estate and property taxes, and strange-sounding taxes like the candle tax and the box tax. Records were also kept of merchants (business owners), and of requests for *mikvah* (Jewish ritual bath) maintenance funds.

A *candle tax* was a tax on Shabbat candles (candles lit when Jews mark the beginning of the Sabbath on Friday night). The money collected was used for Jewish education.

The *box tax* was a tax that was imposed upon the entire Jewish population in Russia. The box tax was a tax on kosher meat, and was also called the "*pushke*" or "*kupah*" tax in Lithuania. (A *pushke* in Yiddish is a small box or can into which people drop coins for charity. A *kupah* in Hebrew is a cash box or basket.) The money collected was used to fund the social obligations of the community, and even to pay the local rabbi's salary.

Voter records from Russia, another valuable tool in your genealogy toolbox, get information from:

- Elector lists (lists of people who are allowed to vote in an election)

- State Duma electors lists (A *duma* is the legislative or ruling body in Russia and some other republics of the former Soviet Union; it is like a congress or parliament)
- Lists of electors of representatives to local municipalities
- Rabbi's Elector lists (The Russian government insisted that a secularly educated rabbi, not the local yeshiva-educated rabbi, keep the *kahal* records. Local residents voted for the local state rabbi.)
- Resident lists

For example, a list of eligible voters (Duma Voter List) from the Russian Empire for the years 1906 and 1907 is available online.

Part of a 1912 list of voters for the State Duma in the Mozyr district of Minsk Gubernia: Voters 527 and 528 are relatives of an author

Information on tax and voter records from various countries can be found on many of the major genealogy websites like ancestry.com, familysearch.org, jewishgen.org, and myheritage.com.

Records such as Merchant Lists (tradespeople in the district) or Craftsmen and Guild Lists were sometimes kept of people in certain professions. Craftsmen and artisans belonged to special guilds (professional organizations), and they were given privileges such as exemption from paying certain taxes.

Often, family members continued in the same craft trades for generations, which makes these lists valuable for genealogy research. You might find out that you come from a long line of woodworkers, or that your great-grandfather and great-great-grandfather were both shop owners! Who knows—maybe you'll end up following in your ancestors' footsteps someday.

In the Ottoman Empire (the area centered around Turkey and the Middle East), tax registers called *tahrir defterleri* were compiled in the 15th and 16th centuries. These lists are still available in archives in Turkey and surrounding countries and online through the Turkish Cultural Foundation at turkishculture.org. The registers list the names, legal status, and number of men in the countries' towns. Obviously you have to know Turkish, written in the Arabic alphabet at that time, to read these.

✡ Ketubot

You may discover a *ketubah* during your searches, either in your home or elsewhere. A *ketubah*, or Jewish marriage contract, can provide valuable tidbits of information about your family history, such as:

- Jewish (and possibly secular) date of wedding
- Location of wedding
- Jewish (and possibly secular) names of bride and groom
- If the father of the bride or groom is a member of the *Kohanim* (ancient High Priests) or *Levi'im* (assistants to the ancient High Priests)
- Jewish names of parent or parents; a *ketubah* from the Sephardic tradition may even list grandparents or earlier ancestors
- Names of the two witnesses who signed the *ketubah* (who may have been distant cousins of the bride or groom, even though relatives are not supposed to be witnesses)

The *ketubah*, which is signed prior to the Jewish marriage ceremony and read aloud under the *chuppah* (marriage canopy), is a Jewish legal document invented in ancient times. The earliest known *ketubah* was created in Egypt about 2,500 years ago, although the current format was created about 2,100 years ago. To this day, it is still written (or printed) in Aramaic, the language that was commonly spoken by Jews living in ancient times, and the language that has always been used for Jewish legal documents.

Your family may have in its possession a relative's fragile *ketubah* from the "Old Country." You may ask to see the *ketubah* so you can copy down the information it contains, and you may even be allowed to take a picture of the certificate, but please handle the *ketubah* carefully. If a Jewish person is married to someone who is not Jewish, a *ketubah* may or may not be available.

Most *ketubot* (plural of *ketubah*) are written according to a strict formula, so if you can read sometimes not-very-neat Hebrew handwriting, you can find out all sorts of fun things:

- The first item is the day of the week, then the Hebrew date, month, and year
- Following that is the city where the wedding occurred
- Then come the Jewish name of the groom, the words "son of," the father's name (and whether the father is a *Kohen* or *Levi*), and the groom's last name

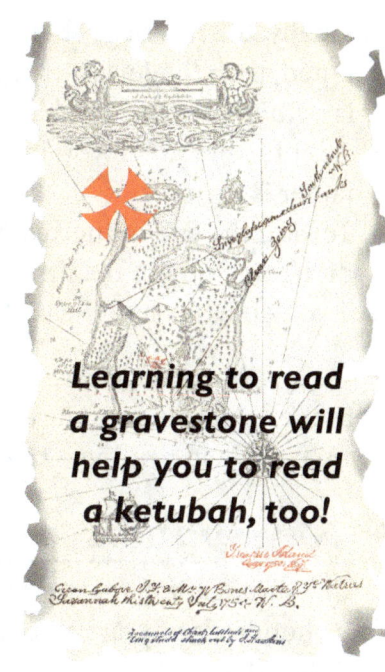

Learning to read a gravestone will help you to read a ketubah, too!

- Day of the week, Hebrew date, month, and year
- Place
- Groom's name
- Bride's name and details
- Whether bride's father is alive or not
- Groom's name
- Bride's name and details
- Witnesses

Ketubah of Stephen Cohen's grandparents

- Finally, the marriage status of the bride (first marriage, widow, divorced) and whether she is a convert is noted, then the Jewish name of the bride is written, as well as her father's name (and whether her father is a *Kohen* or *Levi*), and her last name
- A bit further down you may find the word *nosa* (if the bride's father is not living) or *avuha* (if the bride's father is living)
- Toward the end of the *ketubah*, the full names of the bride and groom are repeated (just in case you didn't catch them the first time!)
- Two witnesses sign the bottom of the *ketubah*; these witnesses are not supposed to be relatives

A Jewish marriage certificate is an important and special document. If you're lucky enough to find one from the "Old Country," just know that its format has remained remarkably the same for hundreds of years. If you need help reading a *ketubah*, contact a genealogist or a rabbi.

✡ Newspapers

Jews were among the few groups of people who could read way back when lands began keeping civil records hundreds of years ago. And when newspapers started in the late 19th century in the Russian Empire, read they did.

Some of Russia's most popular Hebrew and Yiddish newspapers can be found in Tel Aviv University's database, Historical Jewish Press (nli.org.il), mentioned in a previous chapter. Often these newspapers were supported by donations, and one of your relatives may be mentioned in a donation notice. There were also many newspapers for Sephardim in Morocco, Turkey, and other countries.

✡ Military records

If an ancestor or cousin was in the army in the old country, there may be ways to find a record of this military service. Russia, for example, has an interesting online database of military records.

The database (obd-memorial.ru/html) includes soldiers of the Red Army (the military of the Soviet Union, which collapsed in 1991). You will have to read the Cyrillic alphabet, though, and remember the rule of flexibility with names written using various alphabets and spellings.

Two sorts of documents exist in this database:

- Forms for tracking down missing soldiers, which were documents that relatives filled out to try to learn the fates of their loved ones, whether missing or killed in action
- Reports of losses, which were lists created by the military leadership of soldiers who were missing, captured, or killed

There are experts on military history who may be able to tell you, based on the uniform worn by your relative, the corresponding regiment or division of the army. For example, in this book's "Introduction," the picture of the marching band in front of a building is of a Russian regiment stationed in the Ukrainian city of Zhytomyr, dating from the Russo-Japanese War (1904–5). The great-great uncle of Stephen Cohen

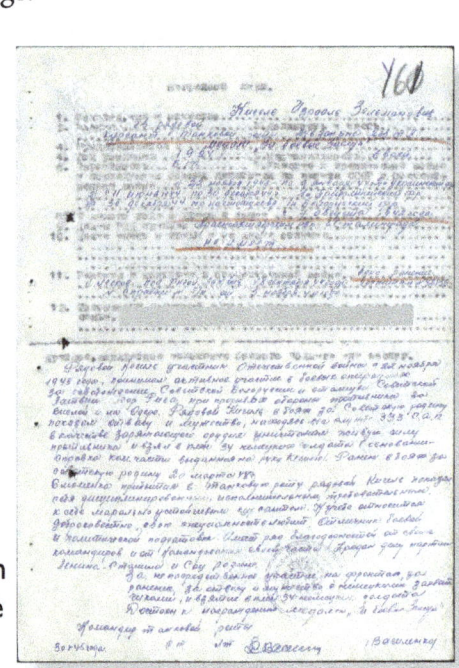

A relative of Stephen Cohen won a military medal from the USSR in World War II: This is the paperwork (in the Russian language) for the medal

is shown under the magnifying glass. He holds a helicon, an instrument similar to a tuba.

✡ Cemeteries

The JewishGen Online Worldwide Burial Registry (JOWBR) at jewishgen.org provides information and records regarding Jewish burials throughout the world. The website mitzvatemet.com/en/burials has an index and images of Jewish graves in Eastern Europe. For information on Jewish graves in Iran, search beheshtieh.com. The website jewishturkstones.tau.ac.il documents Jewish gravestones in the Ottoman Empire and Turkey. The websites billiongraves.com and findagrave.com also have databases of graves throughout the world. Every year, more and more gravestones—old and new—are being photographed and documented in databases, which you can now search. This book's chapter on cemeteries provides hints on how to decipher the writing and symbols on gravestones.

A relative of Stephen Cohen was a Polish soldier in the 1930s; perhaps you can find military records of your relatives from the "Old Country"

Remnants of a Community: The Holocaust

During the Holocaust, which started in the 1930s and ended in 1945, millions of Jewish men, women, and children were killed in Europe, along with non-Jews who had a Jewish ancestor, or who were married to Jews. Also killed were people of an ethnic group, sexual orientation, or political persuasion deemed undesirable by the Nazis. Millions more were imprisoned in concentration camps or ghettos. Some survived the camps and were able to tell the world their stories. Perhaps the most famous chronicler of this destruction was Elie Wiesel (1928–2016), born in Sighet, Romania. Wiesel wrote more than fifty books on the subject, and received the 1986 Nobel Peace Prize.

The utter, deliberate destruction of Jewish life during this era has come to be called the **Holocaust** in English, *Shoah* in Hebrew, and *Khurbn* in Yiddish. You may have relatives who were trapped in camps or ghettos, or were murdered, during this time period. While the Holocaust is a dark moment in Jewish history, it is still a part of our story—perhaps your family's story—and the people who were caught in its grip deserve to be remembered.

Recording your relatives' experiences in the Holocaust is one way to keep alive the memory of those who perished. But how do you do that?

Arbeitsbuch (German for "employment book") from the end of the Holocaust period, for a Jew living in Bohemia and Moravia: Such books were required for proper work documentation in the Nazi empire

★ Yizkor Books

Yizkor Books (*yizkor* means "May [God] remember"), or memorial books, were originally created in Jewish communities as publications in which lists of names, places, and dates could be printed so Jews could say memorial prayers (*Kaddish*) for their relatives. After World War II ended in 1945, however, many Yizkor Books were published by survivors as a way to remember the Jews from their former towns who died during the Holocaust, and the communities that they once called home.

Caryn Alter, one of the authors of this book, owns a copy of a Yizkor Book called *Yampol: A City in Flames* about a town in Ukraine called Yampol, the birthplace of two of her grandparents. Yizkor Books usually provide a history of the town, along with short stories about people who lived there and notable events. These books may even

Yizkor Book about the Jewish community in Yampol, Ukraine

have stories about your relatives, or the names of your family members who were victims of the Holocaust. There may also be a list of people who survived, a directory of the *landsmanshaft* organizations around the world memorializing the town, photographs of people and places in the town, and a map of the town. Even if you don't have relatives who perished in the Holocaust, these books will provide a glimpse of the communities and cultures that were once a part of your ancestors' lives. A Yizkor Book is a valuable resource for discovering relatives, and provides us with a sense of where we came from and why we are the people we are today.

JewishGen has an extensive collection of Yizkor Books. In the mid-1990s, a group of genealogists from jewishgen.org decided to translate into English some of these Yizkor Books that were written in Hebrew and Yiddish. This Yizkor Book Project connected genealogists who were researching the same town, raised funds, found translators, and then posted the Yizkor Book translations on its website: jewishgen.org/yizkor/. Although approximately 2,000 Yizkor Books were written, not all of them have been translated. The translation process is ongoing.

The New York Public Library has a huge online collection of untranslated Yizkor Books at libguides.nypl.org/yizkorbooks. The Yiddish Book Center offers for purchase reprints of Yizkor Books in its collection (yiddishbookcenter.org/collections/yizkor-books).

To locate a Yizkor Book:

1. Find the name and correct spelling of your ancestors' town using JewishGen's "Town Finder" at jewishgen.org/Communities/Search.asp.
2. Go to jewishgen.org/yizkor/, select "Translations" and see if there is a Yizkor Book about your ancestors' town. It may be partially translated, or fully translated and posted on the website.
3. Also check to see if the Yizkor Book was published by JewishGen Press at jewishgen.org/Yizkor/ybip.html.

✡ *Yad Vashem Records*

Yad Vashem is the World Holocaust Remembrance Center and is located in Israel. Since 1955, one of Yad Vashem's missions has been to collect the names of the six million Jews who were killed in the Holocaust in order to preserve their memories. This is called the Shoah Victims' Names Recovery Project. There are still thousands of victims who have not yet been identified.

Yad Vashem collects much of its information through "Shoah Survivors and Refugees Registration Forms" and "Pages of Testimony" that are filled out by Holocaust survivors or their family members.

Source: THE CENTRAL DATABASE OF SHOAH VICTIMS' NAMES, Yad Vashem

This *Daf-Eid* (Page of Testimony), found in the online Central Database of Shoah Victims' Names, memorializes Aron Mittwoch of Lakhva, a small town in southern Belarus: This Page of Testimony was completed by Avraham Shusterman, his relative (both Aron and Avraham Shusterman were cousins of Stephen Cohen)

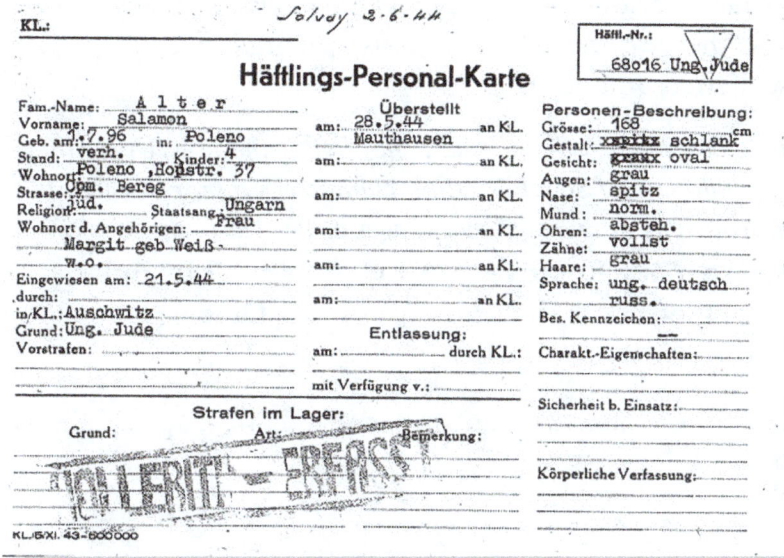

This personal card file from the Mauthausen concentration camp in Austria was written about the grandfather of Caryn Alter's spouse: Salamon (Szulim) Alter survived three concentration camps, and although he lived to see his concentration camp liberated at the end of World War II, he unfortunately died a short while later

Source: THE CENTRAL DATABASE OF SHOAH VICTIMS' NAMES, Yad Vashem

Additional records and an online collection of photos are also available on the Yad Vashem website (yadvashem.org). Caryn Alter was able to find a copy of the concentration camp record that was kept for her husband's grandfather, a grim reminder of his experiences as a Hungarian Jew deported from his home in the 1940s. You may be able to find information about some of your family members as well.

One of the challenges of pinpointing an ancestor's town is that the borders of the countries in Europe changed often, especially during and after wars. For example, a town that could have at one time been in Czechoslovakia, and then in Hungary, might now be in Ukraine.

✸ Other Holocaust Museums, Memorials, and Archives

Based in Washington, D.C., the United States Holocaust Memorial Museum (ushmm.org) memorializes all those murdered in the Holocaust. Its Holocaust Survivors and Victims Database may have documents to help you in your research.

Founded shortly after World War II by the Allies in Germany, the International Tracing Service (ITS) helped families trace their missing relatives. The organization is now called the Arolsen Archives, and has records on millions of victims of Nazi persecution at arolsen-archives.org.

Many other cities and countries around the world also have Holocaust museums and monuments.

✸ Interviews with Family Members

Many Holocaust survivors found it painful to discuss the events of the Holocaust and the actions they had to take in order to survive. But some survivors were anxious to share their stories of survival with the next generation, and may even have provided an account (written or recorded) of their experiences. Another resource is the USC Shoah Foundation's Visual History Archive (sfi.usc.edu), which has a collection of its recorded interviews with Holocaust survivors.

Local or state Holocaust commissions regularly run programs related to the Holocaust. Your local Holocaust commission may even be able to help you search for information.

✸ Survivors' Published Accounts

There are many books (other than Yizkor Books) that tell survivors' stories. Local libraries, archives, and the Internet can help you in your search for these stories. JewishGen Press has published many memoirs, or personal histories, of Holocaust survivors. They are available from jewishgen.org/Yizkor/ybip.html#Memoirs, but check with a parent because they cost money.

Do you have any relatives who died during the Holocaust? List them, where they lived, and how/where they died. If they aren't yet in the Yad Vashem Central Database of Shoah Victims' Names, ask a parent about filling out a Page of Testimony for each person. Attach as many worksheet pages as needed to this book.

Name of Holocaust Victim	Place Where Your Relative Lived	How/Where Your Relative Died

Digging Up Clues from the Land of Israel

✡ Aliyah

ALIYAH IS A HEBREW WORD that means "ascent." It can refer to being "called up" to read from the Torah or to recite the blessings, and it can also mean immigrating, or moving to, Israel.

Although Jews have lived in and moved to this small country bordering the Mediterranean Sea for thousands of years, waves of Jews "made *aliyah*" starting in the 1880s, with the birth of the modern Zionist movement. At that time, the land was within the Ottoman Empire, so many records of that era are likely to be in Turkish. This first wave of about 30,000 Jews came to be known as the *First Aliyah*.

Immigrants (including two young relatives of Stephen Cohen) to Palestine, on the ship *Palestina*, March 1935

Immigration to Israel increased after World War I ended in 1918, when the area became the British Mandate of Palestine. Between 1924 and 1939, about 300,000 Jewish immigrants were able to reach Palestine. Tel Aviv's population, which was not even 4,000 in 1921, soared to 135,000 by 1935.

The Atlit detention camp was built in Palestine by the British and used as a holding camp for illegal Jewish immigrants from 1939 to 1948. These Jewish immigrants were considered to be "illegal" because they did not have official entry permits for immigration. Other illegal immigrants were sent to Cyprus, an island in the Mediterranean Sea, and kept in a detention camp there. Many of the people imprisoned in these camps had fled the Nazi persecution in Europe. Despite many obstacles, Jews continued to make *aliyah* illegally. Today, the Atlit detention camp is a museum located near Haifa in Israel.

The Jewish National Fund and the Society for Preservation of Israel Heritage Sites are working together on a project to learn more about the 130,000

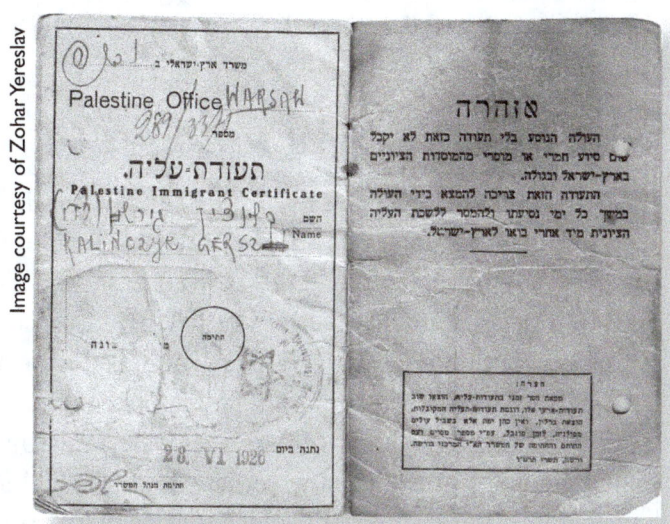

T'udat-Aliya (Palestine Immigrant Certificate), issued in in Warsaw, Poland in 1926 for a Jew leaving for Palestine: The last name and then the first name are written in Hebrew and Polish

immigrants who made *aliyah* during World War II. Oral histories (recorded interviews) of some of these survivors are part of this project. A computerized database and information center at the Atlit "Illegal" Immigrant Detention Camp in Israel (jnf.org/our-work/heritage-site-preservation) will trace thousands of immigrants who entered Palestine from 1934 to 1948. Personal pages and testimonies have been processed and recorded.

After the State of Israel was formed in 1948, a new wave of immigrants arrived from Europe as well as from Arab countries, where antisemitism was increasing. Israel is now home to the largest Jewish community in the world, and some of your family members may be a part of this community. The population includes Jews of Sephardic and Ashkenazic backgrounds, as well as Jews who trace their heritage to many different communities from around the world.

Israel has a treasure trove of resources for junior genealogists. You can feel like an archaeologist researching biblical artifacts as you "unearth" new clues.

Ship manifest for the S.S. *Yerushalayim*, arriving May 14, 1934 in Haifa, with two of Stephen Cohen's relatives on board

✡ Military Records

The Israel Defense Force, Israel's military force, has an online database (in Hebrew) of soldiers killed in action at izkor.gov.il.

Other valuable research websites include Fallen Citizens in the State of Israel (in Hebrew) at laad.btl.gov.il, the Haganah Historical Archives (*Haganah* was the Jewish paramilitary defense organization in Palestine; in Hebrew) at archives.mod.gov.il, the Ghetto Fighters' House Museum (English available on website) at gfh.org.il/eng, and The Paratroops Heritage Association (English available on website) at paratroops.org.il.

✡ Cemeteries and Burial Records

Burial in Israel, especially at the cemetery at *Har HaZeitim* (Mount of Olives) in Jerusalem, is considered important to many Jews. The International Jewish Cemetery Project of the International Association of Jewish Genealogical Societies (IAJGS) has information on cemeteries in Israel (as well as other countries), where some of your relatives might be buried. According to its website, iajgscemetery.org, all cemeteries in Israel are completely digitized. General burial websites like billiongraves.com and findagrave.com may also have information on some of the graves in Israel.

The Israel Genealogy Research Association (IGRA) has a listing in English of the burial societies in Israel at genealogy.org.il. Many cemeteries in Israel have begun to computerize their burial records, and may have a computer at their entrances for use by the public. The JewishGen Online Worldwide Burial Registry (JOWBR) is a computer database with names and gravestone photographs of people buried in Jewish cemeteries in Israel and worldwide (jewishgen.org/databases/Cemetery).

✸ Lists of People

The United States Holocaust Memorial Museum (ushmm.org) has an index of the newspaper *LaKarov v'Larahok*, which was published from 1945 to 1947 by the Jewish Agency's Search Bureau for Missing Relatives, to help people locate towns where Holocaust survivors lived and the names of survivors. The 73 issues of the newspaper contain approximately 300,000 names of Holocaust survivors.

NAME ALERT: Many Jews who immigrated to Israel changed their names to make them more Hebrew-sounding. If your great-grandfather's first name was *Hersh* (Yiddish for "deer") in Poland, it might have become *Zvi* (Hebrew for "deer") in Israel. Surnames (last names) often were changed after arrival in Israel. Stephen Cohen has a relative who changed his last name from Shusterman to Sharon (keeping the Hebrew letters *shin*, *resh*, and *nun* of the Yiddish original name).

There is also a database of United States Department of State Consular Post Records with helpful information about Americans who contacted the United States Government's official representatives in Palestine to apply for passports or to reach relatives in Palestine during an emergency. This was in the days before telephones and the Internet were available, and these records are available online at jewishgen.org/databases/Israel/group84.htm.

✸ Telephone Directories

Israel Phone Book (israelpb.com) is an online telephone directory published in English that lists the telephone numbers of Israeli residences.

✸ Genealogy Societies in Israel

The IGRA (genealogy.org.il) helps members of the Association from Israel and other countries research their family histories by providing many documents and other materials that are only available in Israel. The IGRA has hundreds of records on topics such as census records, donations, education, local and national elections, the Holocaust, immigration, the military, name changes, occupations, sports, and vital records (birth, marriage, death/cemeteries). There is a description of each database in both Hebrew and English. Only people who are logged in (you can register for free) on the Association's website can search the databases.

The Israeli Association for the Study of Family Roots (isragen.org.il; in Hebrew) provides its members with family history research assistance, and the general public with forums geared toward particular countries, cities, languages, and historical periods.

The National Library of Israel (nli.org.il/en), located in Jerusalem, offers assistance to people researching their family histories. This assistance is available free of charge through specially arranged appointments after an online form has been completed.

Beneath the Surface

IMAGINE BEING ON A TREASURE HUNT. To find the hidden treasure, you might have to search in a dusty basement, peek into a cluttered attic, or even dig in the dirt. But it will all be worth it when you find what you're looking for.

Sometimes, in the hunt for genealogical treasures, you might even stumble upon some interesting facts that you weren't expecting. Some of those facts might also come as a surprise (pleasant or otherwise) to your relatives. Here's some advice on when and how to share newly-found family information that may have been hidden beneath the surface for many years.

✡ *Conversion (or Not)*

Conversion means to change from one religion to another. Over thousands of years of Jewish history, many people who were not born Jewish have chosen to convert to Judaism. Perhaps one of the most famous converts to Judaism was Ruth in Biblical times. Ruth, according to the Book of Ruth in the Torah, was a Moabite woman who converted to Judaism after marrying into an Israelite family. She was the great-grandmother of King David.

You might discover, as you interview family members or search online, that some of your relatives were not born Jewish and chose to convert to Judaism. This fact may be known to the entire family, or it may not be common knowledge. If you learn that this fact is not known by other relatives, you may want to ask the person who converted if this information should be made public. It is interesting to note that Jewish tradition is quite clear on the matter of conversion to Judaism: The Talmud (*Bava Metzia* 58b–59b) tells us that we must treat converts to Judaism as completely Jewish, even to the point of not pointing out to other people that they are converts.

On the other hand, you may discover relatives who were born Jewish, and then converted to another religion. This conversion may or may not be common knowledge, and the person who converted should advise you on how to handle this information.

During World War II, many young Jewish children in European countries were brought by their parents to friends, neighbors, or religious organizations who offered to watch and protect the children during the war. These friends, neighbors, and religious organizations were often not Jewish, so these "hidden children" may have lived for a period of time in a non-Jewish environment. If the parents of these children did not survive the war, it's possible that these children may have then grown up without ever realizing that they were born Jewish.

The Spanish Expulsion in 1492 forced practicing Jews to leave Spain. The Jews who remained in Spain either willingly converted to Christianity, or unwillingly converted to Christianity and continued to secretly practice Judaism. *Converso*, *marrano*, *New Christian*, and *crypto-Jew* are some of the names used to describe these Jews. If you are descended from Jews who once lived in Spain and its surrounding areas, this might be part of your family's story as well. The Converso Genealogy Project was launched to create a genealogical database on these families.

During the course of your genealogical journey, you might encounter a relative who married a person who was not born Jewish and who chose not to convert to Judaism. There will be genealogical documents about this non-Jewish relative, but no Jewish birth, marriage, divorce, or death records.

✡ Adoption

In years past, when a baby or child was adopted, the records were often sealed and no one was allowed to look at them. Sometimes that is still true today, although the Internet and changes in the law have made it easier for people who were adopted to locate one or both of their birth (biological) parents.

Babies or children who were not born Jewish, but who were adopted by Jewish families, may have had a Jewish conversion. According to many rabbis, if an adopted child is not definitely known to be Jewish, that child must have a formal conversion in order to be considered Jewish.

Caryn Alter, one of the authors of this book, was asked by a friend for assistance in getting information about his biological mother (the woman who gave birth to him). This friend had been adopted by a Jewish couple in the 1950s when he was an infant; his biological mother was known to be Jewish. Caryn's friend knew the last name of his biological mother, and thought he knew her first name. After looking at census records, telephone directories, and newspaper clippings that were available online at ancestry.com and newspapers.com, Caryn was able to determine the biological mother's correct first name, and the names of her mother, father, and younger brother. She even found the biological mother's photo in a Brooklyn, New York high school yearbook that had been posted online by ancestry.com. This was the first photo that the friend had ever seen of his biological mother!

IMPORTANT: Finding out that someone was adopted could be sensitive information that you should share with others **only** with permission from the person who was adopted. And, in the unlikely event that you discover that someone might be adopted and not realize it, please speak with a parent or other adult before sharing this information with anyone.

Check with your parents before revealing adoption information that you might have discovered.

✡ Criminals in Your Past

Jewish-American gang members and mobsters have been traced back to the late 1800s. Could one of these famous, or not-so-famous, criminals have been part of your family tree? Anything is possible!

Jewish pirates lived in the Caribbean in the 17th century. Jewish mobsters were part of organized crime (illegal activities done by a large group) in the 1920s. You might unearth information about criminal activity in your family background. This could be a topic that family members hesitate to discuss, so handle this information carefully.

Stephen Cohen has a great-grandfather who became a Russian sailor, traveled to Canada, and crossed the border from Canada into the United States without any immigration documents. He never became a citizen of the United States, and was therefore considered an illegal resident of the country. To this day, Stephen has found no definitive record of his great-grandfather's emigration from the Russian Empire to North America.

Crimes that were committed a hundred or more years ago, such as the

"True Crime" alert!

illegal entry into the United States of the Russian sailor, could certainly add some colorful tales to your family history!

Another interesting, yet dark, chapter in American history was the "McCarthy Era," named after Senator Joseph McCarthy. During this period, which spanned the late 1940s through the 1950s, thousands of Americans were accused by McCarthy of being either Communists or supporters of the Communist political system. Many of these American citizens were interviewed and investigated by the United States government or other agencies. Among the primary targets were union activists, government employees, educators, and those in the entertainment industry. Many people lost their jobs, and some were even sent to jail.

If you write to the United States Federal Bureau of Investigation (FBI) under the provisions of the Freedom of Information Act (FOIA), you might uncover some interesting reports like the one Stephen Cohen found for a relative (right). Instructions for making a FOIA request can be found at foia.gov. Spoiler alert: The FBI closed the case on this relative after finding nothing suspicious.

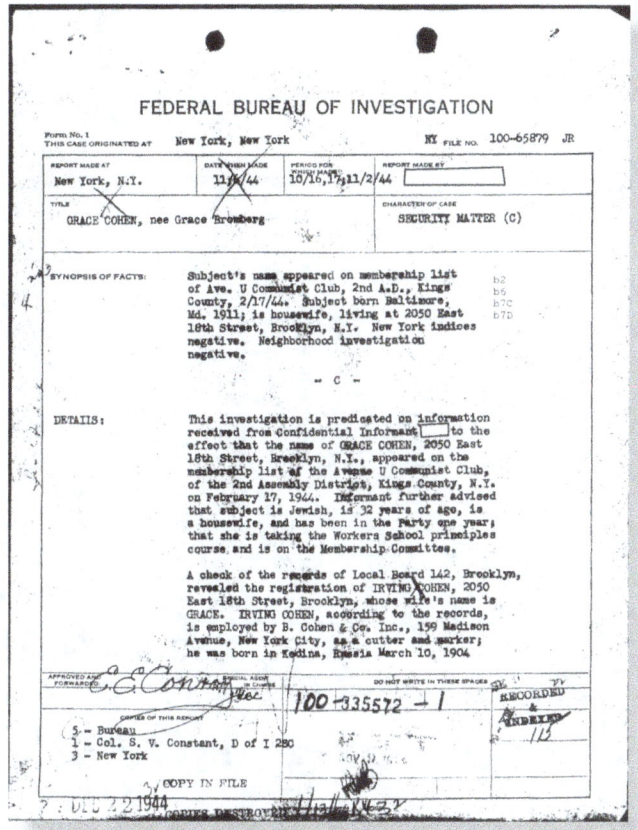

First page of an FBI report

★ Multiple Marriages and Divorce

Family trees can resemble trees that grow in the forest: They can have just a few branches or many branches, and those branches can be fairly straight or elaborately intertwined. It is not uncommon to find family trees that have multiple branches and that may include relatives who married more than once because a spouse died or divorced.

Because of the possibility of multiple branches in a family tree from relatives who have been married more than once, your family tree may include half-brothers, half-sisters, step-parents, and step-children. These family members may have grown up in the same town, or an ocean apart.

Many years ago, people did not live as long as they generally do today. You might discover, as you do your research, that an ancestor's husband or wife died at a fairly young age. The husband or wife may have eventually married again, and may have had children with this new spouse, therefore creating an intertwined branch on your family tree.

A century or so ago, the *shtetls* of Russia and Europe often had small Jewish populations. Transportation from one area of a country to another could be difficult and treacherous. As a result, it was not uncommon for cousins in the same extended family to marry each other (remember the *pedigree collapse* previously mentioned on page 29?), possibly creating another intertwined branch on your family tree.

Sometimes the United States Federal Census records will show when someone has been married more than once. The Census of the United States from 1910, for example, has the code "M2" near the name of one of Stephen Cohen's relatives. If you look carefully at the census record on the next page, you'll see that Line 12, column 8 (marital status) shows that Morris Kantrovitch was in his second marriage in 1910, although the reason for this second marriage is not known.

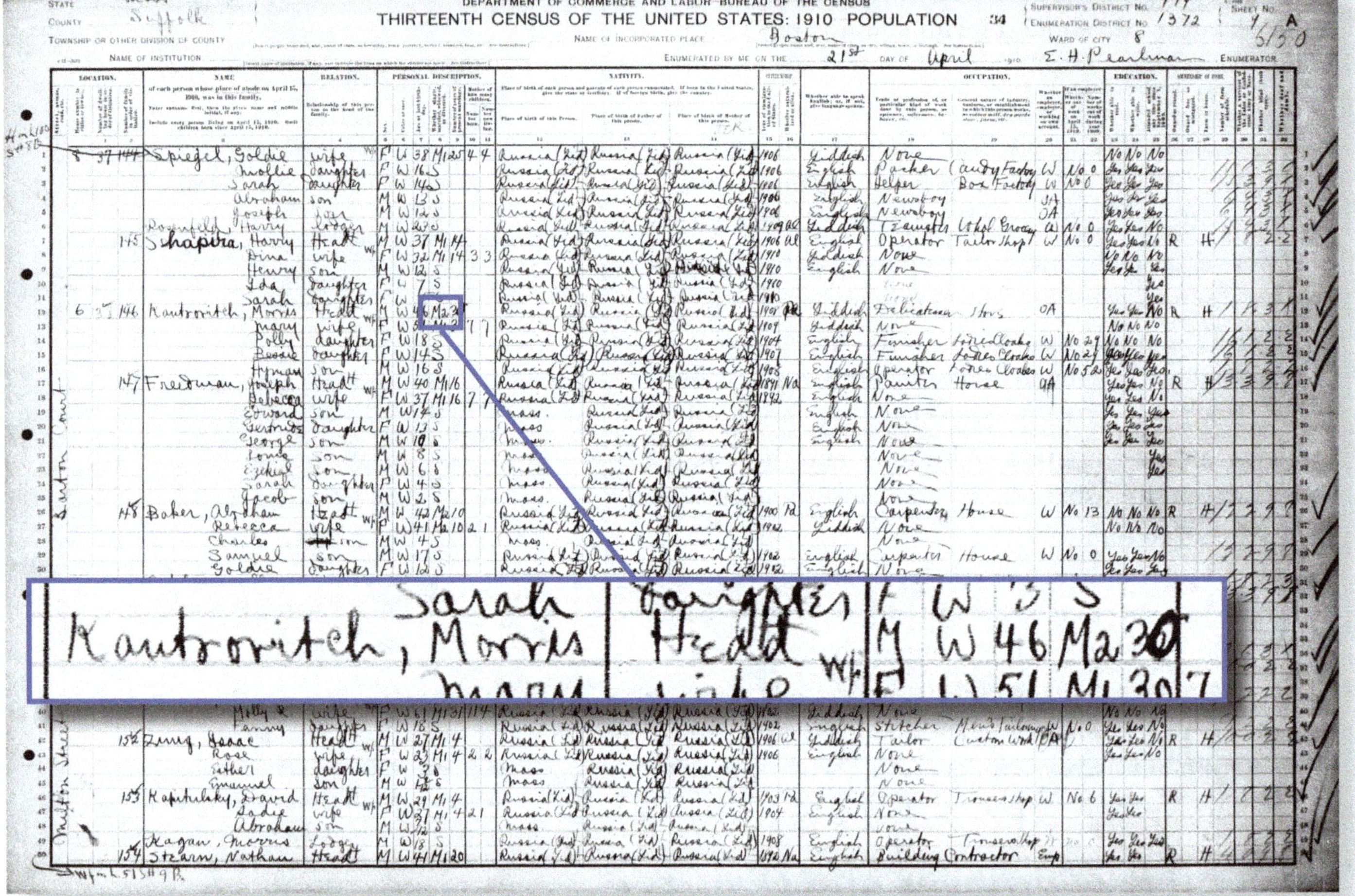

104 Beneath the Surface

1910 Federal Census Record showing Morris Kantrovitch (line 12) and his family:
Column 8 (marital status) reveals M2, a second marriage

There were even some situations, a hundred or more years ago, in which a husband set off to America first in order to earn the money to bring his wife and possibly children over from the "Old Country." Occasionally, the husband's family—for various reasons—never came to the United States. So it's possible that the husband might have eventually married a new wife in this new land. Sometimes the husband came to North America and abandoned his family in Europe, starting a "new life" where no one could find him. As you can imagine, this discovery also needs to be handled carefully.

Another possible explanation for multiple marriages is divorce. Sometimes you will find on marriage certificates that a previous marriage is mentioned.

Divorce documents are discussed in the Torah (*Deuteronomy* 24). The Hebrew word for

Caryn Alter's great-grandparents (both formerly married and then widowed) married each other in Russia in the early 1900s and had additional children together

"divorce document" is *get*. The purpose of a divorce document is to dissolve a marriage entered into "according to the laws of Moses and Israel." It is only required when two people who are Jewish obtain a divorce. Like a *ketubah*, the *get* is in the Aramaic language. A *get* must be handwritten by a scribe.

After a scribe writes a *get*, its four corners are cut off to formalize the divorce. Thus you are unlikely to find a relative's actual *get* to use for research, but your relative may have a *p'tur*, or receipt, noting that the *get* was completed.

If a family member is comfortable with sharing a copy of the *p'tur* with you, it, like any other Jewish document, will provide valuable information for your family tree. Be aware that divorce can be a painful topic, so discuss this information with your family before sharing your research.

Divorce can be a painful topic, so be careful how you handle the information.

✡ The Holocaust

Although there are many books and documentary films about the Holocaust, some survivors found their experiences so harrowing that they chose not to share their memories with friends or relatives. These people or their descendants may not wish to discuss what occurred. Be respectful of their wishes.

✡ Be Considerate

As you have seen from the examples in this chapter, sometimes family history "detectives" have to be careful and considerate when they uncover certain pieces of information during their research. The Yiddish term for being respectful of others is *derekh-eretsdik*. If you're ever unsure whether a fact should be shared with other family members, it's always a good idea to speak with a parent or other adult first, to figure out how to be *derekh-eretsdik*.

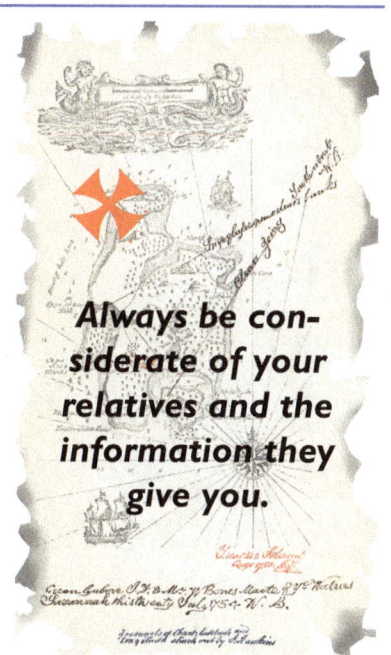

Always be considerate of your relatives and the information they give you.

What Do I Do with It All?

Now that you have begun collecting information about your family, you are probably wondering what to do with all of the documents you find. This is a challenge that many genealogists encounter.

(By the way, for those of you who are interested in chemistry, physics, engineering, and audio recordings, this chapter will be of special interest to you!)

You may choose to scan your relatives' documents, and return the originals to their owners. If someone gave you documents to keep, or you downloaded and printed documents, you may choose to store the paper versions. Or maybe you have a mix of digital files and paper files.

In any case, you want to be sure that these documents don't get lost, destroyed, or damaged over time. You can become the official archivist of the family! An *archivist* is someone who preserves and keeps an archive (a collection of historical documents, images or objects).

Below are some general archive guidelines. You can find more information on successful storage of archival materials at familysearch.org, and you can also check with a professional archivist for specific advice.

✦ Digital Storage

If you store documents on your computer, you should also keep backups of your files (perhaps on discs or thumb drives), and give a copy to a trusted relative who lives in another geographical area. (If there is a fire or flood in your town, you want to be sure that your precious information doesn't get lost.)

Different types of archival digital discs have distinctive features

If you back up your information onto discs, make sure you use archival-quality discs. These are discs made with special materials (often gold-coated) that hopefully will last a hundred years or more. Make sure that you label the discs carefully, using permanent markers only on the side that the computer doesn't read. Don't use adhesive labels, because the glue deteriorates and can damage the disc. Store the discs in special sleeves so they do not get scratched. Keep the discs or thumb drives in a dark, dry, relatively cool (but not cold) area, but never in an attic or basement where they can be exposed to heat and moisture.

Archival discs are more expensive than regular ones. They are available only in specialty shops and on the Internet. Talk to a parent before buying them.

✦ Storing Paper

Most paper and cardboard is made of acidic materials that slowly decompose over time. Therefore, there is only so much you can do to preserve the paper. Some paper is acid-free, but it is not easy to tell.

Put your documents into "archival" photograph storage pages, usually made of polypropylene plastic. Some pages are made of vinyl, which has a distinctive "new car" smell: This odor means there are chemicals that can damage the paper. Never use these kinds of plastic pages—photo pages should have no odor. Many types of storage pages fit into 3-ring binders, like those you take to school.

108   What Do I Do with It All?

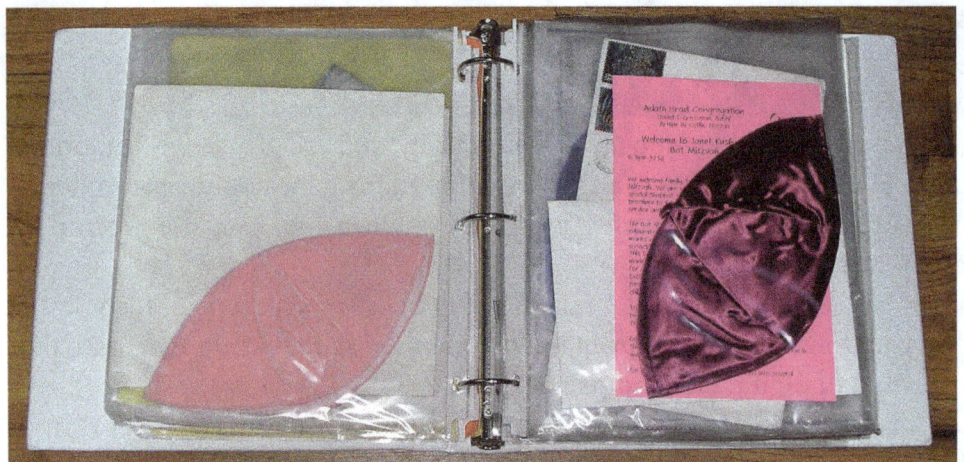

3-ring binder with archival pages to store small documents and objects

Never repair old documents with tape.

Larger documents and thicker objects can be put into heavier archival storage pages and pockets. There are also archival cardboard boxes you can get for storage.

Many photographic shops carry archival pages, and some office supply shops may sell special storage pockets. These are also available online at websites that sell supplies to libraries and archives. Check with a parent before buying these items.

Store your papers in dark, dry, cool places as you would your backup discs. You may notice that many of our relatives' documents shown in this book have yellowish residue from old cellophane tape. Never repair a document with tape: You can see the permanent damage tape will do to paper. If a page is torn, leave it alone.

As mentioned, you may want to scan and digitize your documents.

✦ Storing Photographs

A popular way to store photographs in the 1970s and 1980s was in so-called "magnetic" albums. The pages were not magnetic, but were coated with a light-weight glue that stuck the photographs to the pages. You may find relatives who still store photos in such albums. These albums are very bad for photographs: The glue eventually bonds permanently to the photograph, damaging the photograph's paper. The glue may also decompose, destroying the image on the photograph.

Instead, store your photographs, like documents, in archival photo storage pages in binders or in archival boxes.

Heat, light, and humidity are the enemies when storing important items!

Color images fade with time, and there is little you can do to reverse the damage. All you can do is slow down the process. Black-and-white photographs fade more slowly than color. Store your photographs, like other papers, in dark, cool areas. If you are ambitious, you can carefully scan the photographs and learn to retouch and restore them using image-processing software. There are also companies that can scan your photos for a fee, but check with a parent first about this option.

✴ Movies, Slides, and Negatives

Movies and slides are made of plastic, using special dyes that fade with time. Therefore, you must keep them away from light and heat (which fade them), and humidity/moisture (which allows mold to grow). Like archival photographic pages, there are also archival storage pages for slides.

3-ring binder with archival slide pages

Watch out for "vinegar syndrome" in old movies.

Old movies present a special challenge: Some of the plastic in the movie film, especially from the 1950s and earlier, can decompose, producing a smell like vinegar. People in the movie industry call this "vinegar syndrome." You may have to take a movie with this issue to a special shop that transfers the images to a DVD or thumb drive. If one of your home movies has such an odor, keep it away from the other reels of film.

The different types of plastic in slide and movie film deteriorate at different rates. Nearly all archivists agree that Kodachrome® film is the most durable film for movies and slides…but it is not manufactured anymore.

A local professional photography shop can help you digitize collections of slides and negatives. There are also some companies to which home movies and slides can be mailed to be digitized. Talk to a parent first about either of these options, which can be expensive.

✴ Videotapes and Audio Tapes

Tapes record sounds and pictures on tiny particles of magnetic material glued to the plastic tape. Therefore, the same advice we give for storing other plastic items applies here: Keep old videotapes and audio tapes away from heat, light, and humidity. Glue can deteriorate in heat, causing the magnetic particles to fall off the tape.

There is one other problem: Tapes can be erased by other magnetic fields. If you know a little about physics, you're aware that both magnets and moving electric charges create a magnetic field. So keep all magnets away from tapes. What else can create a magnetic field? Electric motors! Any household object with

A 1970s 8" tape reel: The end of the tape is attached to the reel with an orange clip; this prevents damage to the tape

a motor, which uses a rotating magnetic field, can erase a tape: This means you have to store your tapes away from air conditioners, vacuum cleaners, refrigerators, freezers, window fans, and any other objects with electric motors.

Store all tapes upright (vertical), which is better for the reels. You can also digitize the tapes and make digital files of them, if you have the equipment to play the tapes. Be sure your tape player is properly cleaned and demagnetized before starting.

✦ Vinyl Records

Typical novelty phonograph record that may contain your ancestor's voice

You may even have a few recordings made on old vinyl phonograph records. Sometimes small recording booths were set up as a novelty in amusement parks and fairs up through the 1950s. As with all other plastic materials, keep records away from heat, light, and humidity. Store them upright (vertical) in archival paper sleeves: Laying record albums flat increases the likelihood that they will warp or bend.

If you have the equipment, you can try to digitize these recordings, being careful not to scratch or break the records.

✦ Other Objects

Since you can't fit your ancestor's wine cup or Shabbat candles into a 3-ring binder, store three-dimensional, larger objects in a secure, dust-free cabinet out of direct sunlight. Talk to an antiques expert about how to care for large posters and paintings, and objects that rust, oxidize, fade or corrode, such as silver, copper, iron, and brass.

✦ Be the Archivist!

You have undertaken, using genealogy, the precious task of keeping your heritage alive. Right now, you are still in school, but someday you may have children or other family members with whom you'll want to share all the interesting stories you have uncovered. The documents and other treasured objects you save now will help you to preserve your family history! Talk to a local archivist if you have more questions about rescuing and storing your family's heirlooms.

Part of the genealogical archive of Stephen Cohen: There are 3-ring binders with documents, articles, and photographs, and a shelf of CDs

Where Do I Go from Here?

You've interviewed some relatives, created some family charts, and studied some historical documents. What do you do next?

✦ Meet Other Genealogists

Seek out other genealogists. As we suggested earlier in the book, find a local genealogy club, especially a Jewish genealogy club. These club members have years of experience doing the same thing you do. They have overcome, in many cases, significant challenges in the search for relatives. They may be able to interpret or read a document written in a strange language. They may know of a small town in Slovenia or Poland that you just discovered. They may even be distant relatives of yours! It's also cool to know that you have joined a world-wide club whose members are ready and willing to help you on your journey into the past.

Although there are fewer Jewish genealogy journals than there once were, you may be able to get access to newsletters published by some of the larger Jewish genealogy societies in the United States and other countries. One of the benefits of belonging to a Jewish genealogy society is receiving its newsletter or magazine (usually online these days) with research tips and up-to-date news about genealogy. Perhaps one of your parents would consider paying for a Jewish genealogy society membership, if a student membership is not available, to obtain access to its publications. You will see how deeply some people get involved in genealogy, and all the different reasons genealogy excites them!

✦ Tell Your Relatives

Let your own relatives know that you are now the family historian. They may find more documents or objects related to your family tree. They may suddenly remember stories about the family based upon information you discovered. Their stories will no doubt lead to new questions for you to try to answer. Stephen Cohen sends out an annual newsletter to many family members describing his yearly genealogy findings.

✦ Register at JewishGen

Register your genealogical research interests for free on two main databases at jewishgen.org. Registering at JewishGen is free, and provides you with more access to the website than if you're not registered.

- The Jewish Genealogy Family Finder is a database of genealogists interested in particular surnames (last names) and towns of origin. If your ancestors' town of origin was small, it's possible that many families from that town had intertwined family trees.
- The Family Tree of the Jewish People is a database of family trees that genealogists have uploaded that enables you to search for matches with your family. You need to have genealogy software in order to upload a common genealogy format known as GEDCOM, which allows you to create a family tree that cannot be edited or changed by anyone else. Please ask a parent to help you with this task.

For both databases, you can contact other researchers whose genealogy information matches yours. Subscribe to the JewishGen Discussion Group, which provides daily summaries of genealogy topics and discussions via email. Every day, genealogists both new and experienced ask for advice or help from other members of the discussion group.

✡ Attend a Conference

Attend, with a parent or other family member, a conference sponsored by the International Association of Jewish Genealogical Societies (IAJGS). Its website is iajgs.org. This huge yearly meeting is held at various locations around the world. There you can meet genealogists with shared interests, and attend presentations on the latest research. There is truly nothing like being surrounded by an ocean of Jewish genealogists, and being able to talk with them about your family and theirs. There may also be local Jewish genealogy conferences sponsored by societies in your geographic area. Registration for conferences costs money, so talk to a parent about this choice.

✡ Submit a Page of Testimony

In a previous chapter, we mentioned Yad Vashem as an important source of information about relatives who died during the Holocaust. If, during your research, you discover relatives who lost their lives during this dark time and aren't listed in Yad Vashem's database, fill out a Page of Testimony for each of them at yadvashem.org and submit those pages to Yad Vashem.

✡ Take Stock of Your Work

Remember that sometimes, despite all your research, you might hit a dead end. With the passage of time, information does get lost now and then. Accept that—for now—there are some paths in your research that you cannot pursue. Once in a while you might even meet a relative who refuses to answer your questions. Perhaps later in your life you will acquire the tools, gain the experience, or find the documents you don't have yet to navigate around that dead end. Be patient.

✡ Lekh L'kha (Go Forth)

As Rabbi Hillel said over two thousand years ago, "If I am not for myself, who will be for me? But if I am only for myself, who am I? If not now, when?" (*Pirkei Avot* 1:14) Your task, in the spirit of *tikkun olam* (repairing the world), is to repair and reconstruct your family history, starting now!

Continuing the Journey
✡ What's in a Name?

"A person has three names: one that he is called by his father and mother, one that people know him by, and one that he acquires for himself. The earned name is worth much more than the given name."

(*Ecclesiastes Rabbah* 7:1–4)

Although this book has come to an end, we hope that your genealogy journey will continue for many years to come.

Everyone's family history is unique, and your name is a link to that history. Your name is a special part of who you are, just like the color of your hair or the sound of your voice.

Jewish tradition abounds with references to "names." And according to that tradition, having a "good name" or a "good reputation" is most important of all. As we discussed in previous chapters of this book, speaking with your family members, and showing an interest in their lives, can truly be a mitzvah. Genealogy is a gift that you give to them, as well as to yourself.

We all view the world through our own "lens." As it says in *Pirkei Avot* 3:1, "Know where you came from and where you are going." When we learn about our heritage and our past, it allows us to "see" the present in a different light. We soon realize that our lives are part of a fascinating historical tapestry that is still being woven.

The stories of the family members who came before us can live on in us and in our relatives—but only if we take the time to gather and cherish those stories. So keep searching, keep digging, keep asking, and know that for "history detectives," there is always another piece of the puzzle waiting to be discovered.

Appendix: Resources for Research

THIS APPENDIX IS A SAMPLING, not a complete list, of helpful resources for genealogy research. (Listing of a book or website does not imply our endorsement of it.)

✡ Books

Author	Title	What's in it
Alexander Beider	A Dictionary of Jewish Surnames from the Russian Empire	Origin of over 70,000 family names of Jews who lived in the Russian Empire
	Jewish Surnames in Prague (15th–18th centuries)	Listing of Jewish family names in the city of Prague in the Czech Republic
	A Dictionary of Jewish Surnames from the Kingdom of Poland	Thousands of Jewish family names from the Kingdom of Poland
	A Dictionary of Ashkenazic Given Names	Origin of 15,000 first names of Ashkenazic Jews
	A Dictionary of Jewish Surnames from Galicia	Origin of 25,000 Jewish family names from southwestern Poland and western Ukraine
	A Dictionary of Jewish Surnames from Maghreb, Gibraltar, and Malta	Origin of thousands of Jewish family names from northern Africa, Gibraltar, and the island of Malta
	A Dictionary of Jewish Surnames from Italy, France and "Portuguese" Communities	Origin of thousands of Sephardic family names
Jeffrey S. Malka	Sephardic Genealogy: Discovering Your Sephardic Ancestors and Their World	Guide to Sephardic Jewish genealogy
Lars Menk	A Dictionary of German-Jewish Surnames	Listing of 13,000 Jewish family names from the German Empire
Elizabeth Shown Mills	Evidence! Citation & Analysis for the Family Historian	Details on how to cite your research, and analyze documents for their reliability
Neil Rosenstein	The Unbroken Chain: Biographical Sketches and Genealogy of Illustrious Jewish Families from the 15th–20th Century	Detailed genealogy of many rabbinical families from the Renaissance onward (multiple volumes)
Josef Rosin	Preserving Our Litvak Heritage	History of Jewish communities in Lithuania (3 volumes)
Mathilde A. Tagger	Dictionary of Bulgarian Jewish Surnames	Origin of over 800 Jewish Bulgarian surnames

116   Appendix: Resources for Research

Author	Title	What's in it
Jonathan D. Shea and William F. Hoffman	*Following the Paper Trail: A Multilingual Translation Guide*	Guide to translating various civil records of European countries into English

Many of these books are expensive, but are valuable references for your genealogy journey. See if your local library has them. If not, request to borrow a copy through interlibrary loan (a librarian can show you how to do this). You may also find used copies available for a cheaper price. The books listed above can be purchased at websites like amazon.com, abebooks.com, avotaynu.com/books, barnesandnoble.com, books.google.com, jewishgen.org, and thriftbooks.com.

✡ Websites to Try

Site	What it is	Important notes
a860-historicalvitalrecords.nyc.gov/search	Search for older birth, marriage, and death records in New York City	Free
ajgs.org.au	Australian Jewish Genealogical Society, with information about Jews in Australia	Free
amia.org.ar	*Asociación Mutual Israelita Argentina*, the organization of Jews in Argentina	Free
ancestry.com	Large online database of genealogy records from around the world	Costs money; check if your local library has free access to this website
archive.org	Internet Archive, an online repository of documents and books	Free
archive.org/details/brooklynpubliclibrary?&sort=date	Old telephone books from the Borough of Brooklyn in New York City	Free
archives.gov	United States National Archives and Records Administration (NARA) holdings, including naturalization records	Free
archives.jdc.org	Archives of the American Jewish Joint Distribution Committee, with case files	Free
archives.mod.gov.il	Archives for the History of the Haganah (Jewish paramilitary organization in the British Mandate for Palestine)	Free
archiwa.gov.pl	Polish State Archives, including many Jewish civil records from the 19th and early 20th centuries	Free
arolsen-archives.org/en/	Arolsen Archives website, for finding survivors and victims of Nazi persecution	Free

Appendix: Resources for Research

Site	What it is	Important notes
beheshtieh.com	Jewish gravesites in Iran	Free
billiongraves.com	Billion Graves, a large worldwide database of graves of all religions	Free
bklyn.newspapers.com	Brooklyn Public Library's online database of newspapers in Brooklyn, New York, especially the *Brooklyn Eagle*	Free
cdec.it	Fondazione Centro di Documentazione Ebraica Contemporanea, a site describing the Jewish community of Italy (in Italian)	Free
cemla.com/buscador	CEMLA, the *Centro de Estudios Migratorios Latinoamericanos*, with a database of immigrants to Argentina (in Spanish)	Free
cjh.org	Center for Jewish History: Offices for American Jewish Historical Society, American Sephardi Federation, Leo Baeck Institute, Yeshiva University Museum, and YIVO Institute for Jewish Research	Free
cjhn.ca	The Canadian Jewish Heritage Network, with databases of Canadian Jewish archival documents	Free
consistoire.org	Website for the Jewish community of Paris, *Le Consistoire de Paris*	Free
coraweb.com.au	Information about genealogy research in Australia and elsewhere	Free
deathindexes.com	Death indexes and records from the USA	Free
digitalarchives.bt.com/Calmview/	Information about British Telecom's archives of telecommunications	Free
familysearch.org	Large online genealogy database maintained by The Church of Jesus Christ of Latter-day Saints of records from around the world; has tips on storing historical materials	Free, but registration is required to search databases
farhi.org/genealogy/index.html	*Les Fleurs de l'Orient*'s website on Sephardic genealogy	Free
findagrave.com	Database of cemeteries around the USA, with information (and often photographs) of gravestones	Free
fold3.com	Military records of the USA, UK, and other English-speaking countries	Costs money

Appendix: Resources for Research

Site	What it is	Important notes
freebmd.org.uk	Database of British civil records; work is ongoing	Free
fultonhistory.com	Digitized North American newspapers and postcards, mostly from the area in and around New York State	Free
genealogybank.com	Digitized U.S. newspapers from 1690 to the present	Costs money
genealogyindexer.org/directories	Yizkor Books and directories from around the world	Free
genealogy.org.il	The Israel Genealogy Research Association, with databases on Israel, other countries, and burial societies in Israel	Free, but requires registration
genealoj.org/fr	*Cercle de Généalogie Juive*, Jewish genealogical society of France (Fun fact: In French, the letter "J" is pronounced "zhee," so the website "genealoj" is a pun on the French word *généalogie*)	Free
geshergalicia.org	Organization for research on Jews of Galicia, in the former Austro-Hungarian Empire	Free
gfh.org.il/eng	Ghetto Fighters' House Museum website, with information on Jewish life before, during, and after WWII	Free
gro.gov.uk	United Kingdom's General Record Office index of older birth and death records	Free, but registration is required to search databases
guides.loc.gov	Online research guides for the United States Library of Congress	Free
hebcal.com	Online Jewish calendar with conversions to and from the secular calendar	Free
iajgs.org	International Association of Jewish Genealogical Societies, which sponsors annual international genealogy conferences; some reference information on website	Costs money to attend conferences
iajgscemetery.org	International Association of Jewish Genealogical Societies' cemetery project database	Free
ijarchive.org	The Iraqi Mukharabat Archive of Jewish Materials, on the history of Iraqi Jews	Free
instituteofjewishexperience.org/ancestral-search/	Database for Crypto-Jewish and Sephardic materials	Free

Appendix: Resources for Research

Site	What it is	Important notes
israelpb.com	Online Israeli telephone directory	Free
isragen.org.il	Israeli Association for the Study of Family Roots (in Hebrew)	Free, but registration is required to search databases
italian-family-history.com/jewish/genealogy.html	Website on Jewish genealogy in Italy	Free
italiangen.org	New York City-related databases of birth, marriage, and death indexes up to 1937, plus military, naturalization, and ship records; run by the Italian Genealogical Group	Free
izkor.gov.il	Israeli Defense Force's memorial to fallen soldiers (in Hebrew)	Free
jewishgen.org	Comprehensive source of information on Jewish genealogy, with databases on *shtetls*, translations of Yizkor Books, indexes of vital records, and other records of Jews around the world	Free, but requires registration
jewishgen.org/databases/Cemetery	Large online database of graves in Jewish cemeteries called the JewishGen Online Worldwide Burial Registry (JOWBR)	Registration not required, but increases access to website
jewishgen.org/databases/jeffmalka	Sephardic online database	Free, but requires registration
jewishroots.uct.ac.za	SA Jewish Rootsbank website, with databases related to South African Jewry	Free
jewishturkstones.tau.ac.il	Database of Jewish gravestones in the Ottoman Empire and Turkey	Free
jgs-montreal.org	Jewish Genealogical Society of Montréal, with many databases related to Canadian Jewry	Free
j-italy.org	A collection of websites dedicated to the Jewish communities in Italy	Free
jri-poland.org	Databases and indexes related to Jews of Poland; one of the largest Jewish genealogical databases in the world	Free, but requires registration
laad.btl.gov.il	Fallen citizens in the State of Israel database (in Hebrew)	Free

Site	What it is	Important notes
library-archives.canada.ca/eng	Various Canadian genealogy records from the Library and Archives Canada	Free
litvaksig.org	Website for the Litvak Special Interest Group, which researches Jewish genealogy in Lithuania	Costs money for access to the latest indexes and data
loc.gov/rr/european/tel.html	United States Library of Congress's extensive database of European address and telephone directories	Free
mitzvatemet.com/en/burials	Index and images of Eastern European Jewish gravesites	Free
myheritage.com	Large online database of many types of records from around the world	Costs money; check if your local library has free access to this website
naa.gov.au	National Archives of Australia, including military, citizenship, and census records	Free
nationalarchives.gov.uk	National Archives of London, the storehouse of British civil records	Free
nationalarchives.gov.za	National Archives & Records Service of South Africa	Free
newspaperarchive.com	Digitized U.S. and world newspaper articles	Costs money
newspapers.com	Digitized U.S. newspaper articles	Costs money
nli.org.il/en	National Library of Israel's databases and The Central Archives for the History of the Jewish People	Free
nypl.org	New York Public Library's website, with digitized Yizkor Books	Free
obd-memorial.ru/html	Database of soldiers in the Soviet Union's Red Army (in Russian)	Free
onlysimchas.com	Collection of Jewish births, marriages, and other events from the 21st century	Free
paratroops.org.il	Paratroops Heritage Association, memorializing Israeli paratroopers	Free
patents.google.com	Collection of patents from all over the world	Free
readcoop.eu/transkribus/	Transkribus, an AI program that assists with deciphering handwriting	Free

Site	What it is	Important notes
recherche-collection-search.bac-lac.gc.ca/eng/Census/Index	Library and Archives Canada's census records	Free
reclaimtherecords.org	Reclaim the Records releases and digitizes United States local and state civil records	Free
rtrfoundation.org	Miriam Weiner Routes to Roots Foundation, with Eastern European Archival Database	Free
sephardicgen.com	Genealogy related to Sephardic Jews	Free
sfi.usc.edu	USC Shoah Foundation, with collections of interviews with Holocaust survivors	Free
statueofliberty.org	Database of immigrants who entered the USA through Ellis Island in New York Harbor; also includes photographs and information about the steamships on which they traveled	Free, but requires registration to access all information
stevemorse.org	Steve Morse's One-Step Webpages: Search engine that reaches into other databases and accesses information more easily than the original databases. (Fun fact: The creator of the site, Dr. Steve Morse, is not only a Jewish genealogist, but helped invent the first microprocessor chip for personal computers)	Free, but you must be a member of any fee-based websites it searches
telexplorer.com.ar	Online telephone directory for Argentina	Free
timesmachine.nytimes.com/browser	Archives of all *New York Times* newspapers since 1851	Costs money (subscription to the newspaper)
turkishculture.org	Holdings of the Turkish Cultural Foundation (may contain political propaganda)	Free
ukcensusonline.com	Census records of the United Kingdom	Costs money
uk.wikisource.org/wiki/Архів:Єврейське_містечко	Alex Krakovsky's wiki site with thousands of images from Ukrainian Jewish record books (in Ukrainian)	Free
ushmm.org	U.S. Holocaust Memorial Museum website, including documents and photographs	Free

Site	What it is	Important notes
yadvashem.org	Central repository for information on people killed during the Holocaust; includes a large database of victims' names	Free
yiddishbookcenter.org/collections/yizkor-books	Online repository of Yizkor Books	Free
yivo.org	YIVO Institute for Jewish Research, which researches and collects materials related to the Jews of Eastern Europe (pronounced YEE-voh)	Free

 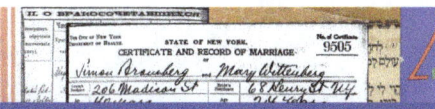 

Words to Know

Alien	A person who is not a citizen of the country in which they are living.
Aliyah	Hebrew: ascent. In a genealogical context, moving to the land of Israel.
Ancestry chart	A genealogical chart showing all the ancestors of a particular person.
Aramaic	Language spoken by Jews about two thousand years ago; similar to Hebrew.
Archive	A collection of documents that supply information.
Ashkenazim	Hebrew: Jews whose ancestors lived in Central and Eastern Europe.
Autosomal DNA test	A DNA test that analyzes the 22 non-sex chromosomes for characteristic sequences.
Beta Israel	Jews whose ancestors lived in Ethiopia.
Birth certificate	A government-issued document certifying the birth of a person.
Brit Milah	Hebrew: Covenant of circumcision. Jewish baby boys are circumcised at the age of 8 days in a special ceremony, at which they are given their Jewish name. In Yiddish it is known as a "bris."
Census	A governmental count of a population.
Chevra kadisha	Aramaic: Holy society. A group of Jews who prepare a dead person for burial.
City directory	A directory listing people, their professions, and addresses in a particular city.
Cyrillic alphabet	Alphabet used by speakers of Russian, Ukrainian, and several other languages in Eastern Europe. (Fun fact: The Cyrillic letter sha ш is derived from the Hebrew letter ש shin.)
Death certificate	A government-issued document certifying the death of a person.
Descendant chart	A genealogical chart showing all the descendants of a particular person.
DP camp	"Displaced Persons" camp. A temporary settlement set up after World War II where refugees stayed until they found homes.
Dzhudezmo	Language related to Spanish and spoken by Sephardic Jews; also called Ladino.
Ellis Island	The most important (but not the only) port of entry for immigrants to the USA between 1892 and 1953; an island in New York Harbor. (Fun fact: Part of the small island is within New Jersey, and part is within New York State. Dispute over which states owned which parts of the island reached the U.S. Supreme Court in 1998.)
Galitsyaner	Yiddish: An Ashkenazic Jew from southeastern Europe who speaks Yiddish with a characteristic dialect.
Get	Aramaic: Jewish divorce document. Plural: Gittin.
Gubernia	Russian: A province of the Russian Empire.

Kahal	Hebrew: Before World War I, the name of the Jewish community's ruling body in European towns.
Ketubah	Hebrew: Jewish marriage contract. Plural: Ketubot.
Khurbn	Yiddish: Holocaust
Kipah	Hebrew: Skullcap, head-covering worn by many Jewish men and sometimes Jewish women. Plural: Kipot.
Kohen	Hebrew: A member of the Jewish priestly class, who performed sacrifices in the Temple in Jerusalem. Pural: Kohanim.
Ladino	Another name for Dzhudezmo, a language similar to Spanish spoken by Sephardic Jews.
Landsmanshaft	Yiddish: A mutual aid society formed by Jews who came from the same town or area in Eastern Europe. Plural: Landsmanshaftn.
Levi	Hebrew: A member of the Jewish class of priestly assistants, who helped the Kohanim in the Temple in Jerusalem. Plural: Levi'im.
Litvak	Yiddish: An Ashkenazic Jew from northeastern Europe who speaks Yiddish with a characteristic dialect.
Magen David	Hebrew: Shield of David. Six-pointed star that became a common symbol of Judaism starting around the 17th century.
Marriage certificate	A government-issued document certifying the marriage of two people.
Matronymic	A name that includes the person's mother's name, e.g., Rivka bat Rachel. (Interesting fact: In the Mi Shebeirach, the prayer for healing, Jews traditionally use a person's matronymic.)
Matzeva	Hebrew: Gravestone. Plural: Matzevot.
Microfilm	Photographic film that stores miniature images of documents.
Mitochondrial DNA test	A DNA test that analyzes the mitochondrial DNA (passed from mother to all children) for characteristic sequences.
Mizrahi	Hebrew: Jews whose ancestors lived in the Middle East.
Mutual aid society	An organization chartered to help support its members with money or with other aspects of daily life when needed.
Naturalization	The process of becoming a citizen of a country.
Naturalization certificate	A government-issued document certifying that a person has become a citizen of a country.
Page of Testimony	A form that can be submitted to Yad Vashem to memorialize a Jew who was killed during the Holocaust.
Pale of Settlement	The western part of the Russian Empire where Jews were allowed to live.
Passport	Government-issued document certifying the holder's identity and citizenship, entitling the person to travel to another country (Some countries also use "internal passports," documents people need to travel within their own country).
Patronymic	A name that includes the person's father's name, e.g., Shmuel ben Rafael.

Pedigree collapse	When the calculated number of someone's ancestors far exceeds the actual number of ancestors, because ancestral relatives married each other.
Port of entry	An entry point at a border, or an actual port on the ocean, through which people enter a country.
Probate	Proving in court that a will is valid, or deciding what to do with a deceased person's property if there is no will.
Reb	Hebrew: A title, similar to "Mr." in English, given to Jewish men. It does not signify a Rabbi.
Sephardim	Hebrew: Jews whose ancestors lived in Spain and Portugal before 1500.
Shidekh	Yiddish: A match of potential partners for marriage. Plural: Shidukhim.
Ship manifest	Detailed listing of people traveling on a particular ship.
Shoah	Hebrew: Holocaust.
Shtetl	Yiddish: Small town. Yiddish plural: Shtetlekh.
Social Security Death Index	An index of death records created from the U.S. Social Security Administration's Death Master File.
Special Interest Group	Group of genealogists who have a particular research area in common. Often abbreviated as SIG.
Vital record	Government record of an important event in a person's life, such as birth, marriage, and death.
Voter List	List of people who are eligible to vote.
Will	A document of instructions for what to do with one's property after one's death.
Yahrzeit	German/Yiddish: Death anniversary. A yahrzeit chart lists the secular dates for a person's death anniversaries in the coming years.
Yarmulke	Yiddish: Skullcap, head-covering worn by many Jewish men and sometimes Jewish women.
Y-DNA test	A DNA test that analyzes the Y-DNA (passed from father to sons) for characteristic sequences.
Yeshiva	A Jewish school, college, or seminary
Yiddish	Language related to German, spoken by Ashkenazic Jews.
Yizkor	Hebrew: May [God] remember. A Yizkor Book is a memory book describing the Jewish life in a town before and during the Holocaust.

A

a860-historicalvitalrecords.nyc.gov/search, 116
abjad, 31, 32
acronym, 22
adoption, 102
airplane manifest, 78
ajgs.org.au, 59, 116
aleph-lamed ligature, 55
Alex Krakovsky, 65, 121
Algeria, 64
aliens, 60, 78
aliyah, 97, 98, 123
    First, 97
All-Russia Census of 1858, 85
alphabets
    Arabic, 88
    Cyrillic, 3, 33, 72, 90, 123
    Greek, 33
    Hebrew, 1, 31, 32, 33, 50, 51, 52, 53, 99
    Roman, 33, 72
    Russian, 21
Alsace, 64
    Census of the Jews of, 1784, 64
American Jewish Joint Distribution Committee, 82, 116
American Ladino League, 33
Amérika, La, 48
amia.org.ar, 66, 116
ancestry chart, 6, 7
ancestry.com, 38, 40, 42, 44, 46, 64, 65, 71, 78, 82, 86, 88, 102, 116
Andorra, 23
announcements
    bar or bat mitzvah, 48
    birth, 48
    death, 47, 48
Arabic
    alphabet, 88
    language, 19, 22, 31, 55
    names, 19
Aramaic, 23, 32, 33, 89, 105, 123
archival
    boxes, 108
    discs, 107
    pages, 108, 109
    paper sleeves, 110
archive, 85, 107, 110, 116
archive.org, 86, 116
Archives
    Arolsen, 95, 116
    Central, for the History of the Jewish People, 82, 120
    for the History of the Haganah, 116
    Library and, Canada, 60, 120, 121
    National, of Australia, 60, 120
    National, of Hungary, 65
    National, of London, 120
    of the American Jewish Joint Distribution Committee, 116
    Polish State, 63, 85, 116
    United States National, and Records Administration (NARA), 116
archives.gov, 39, 116
archives.jdc.org, 82, 116
archives.mod.gov.il, 98, 116
archivist, 107, 110
archiwa.gov.pl, 63, 85, 116
Argentina, 66, 117
Arolsen Archives, 95, 116
arolsen-archives.org, 95, 116
artificial intelligence, 15, 35
Ashkenazim, 14, 20, 21, 22, 23, 32, 63, 66, 67, 81, 82, 98, 115, 123, 124, 125
Atlit detention camp, 97
audio
    recordings, 8, 9, 10, 12, 107, 109
    tapes, 109
Aufbau, 48
Australia, 59, 60, 61, 116, 117, 120
    National Archives of, 60, 120
Australian
    Electoral Rolls, 61
    Jewish Genealogical Society, 61, 116
Austria, 63, 64, 81, 82, 85, 95
Austro-Hungarian Empire, 81, 82, 85
    census, 85
autograph books, 43
autosomal DNA, 16, 123
awards, 10, 12

B

baby-naming certificates, 10
back-of-the-envelope calculation, 28
bar and bat mitzvah, 9, 10, 12, 48
    announcements, 48
    certificates, 12
beheshtieh.com, 57, 91, 117
Beider, Alexander, 115
Belarus, 14, 56, 73, 77, 84, 85, 94
Belgium, 63, 70, 77
Bene Israel, 83
Bessarabia, 66
Beta Israel, 23, 83, 123
Bevis Marks Synagogue, 61
Billion Graves, 117
billiongraves.com, 57, 91, 98, 117
birth
    announcements, 48
    certificates, 9, 12, 40, 61, 85, 123
    dates, 5, 6, 9, 25
    indexes, 61, 64, 65
    notices, 47
    places, 5, 6, 9, 10, 25, 26, 27, 44, 46, 93
    records, 61, 65, 67, 85, 99, 134
bklyn.newspapers.com, 48, 117
bobeh-mayseh, 71
books, 54
border crossing records, 67, 77
box tax, 87
Brazil, 66
bride, 13, 88, 89, 90
British
    Commonwealth, vi, 59, 61
    Empire, 59
    Telecom Archives, 62
brit milah, 10, 12, 83
    certificates, 12
Brooklyn Eagle, 117
Brooklyn Public Library, 86, 117
Bulgarian, 33, 115
business directories, 65, 86
    Carpathian Ruthenia, 1925, 86
    Poland, 86

C

calendar
    Hebrew, 51, 53
Canada, 59, 60, 61, 66, 69, 72, 77, 102, 120, 121
    Library and Archives, 60, 120, 121
Canadian
    Jewish Heritage Network, 59, 61, 117
    Jewish Name Research, 61
candle tax, 87
Carpathian Ruthenia Business Directory, 1925, 86
carvings of animals (on gravestones), 54
cause of death, 40
cdec.it, 83, 117
cemeteries, 5, 6, 11, 12, 17, 27, 42, 44, 49, 50, 51, 52, 53, 54, 55, 56, 57, 58, 66, 73, 98, 99, 117, 118, 119, 120
    maps, 12, 58
cemla.com/buscador, 66, 117
census, 37, 38, 42, 60, 61, 65, 67, 82, 85, 99, 102, 103, 120, 121
    All-Russia of 1858, 85
    Austro-Hungarian Empire, 85
    Jews of Alsace, 1784, 64
    records, 37, 38, 60, 85
    United States Federal, 37, 38, 103
    United States State, 38
Center for Jewish History, 117
Central Archives for the History of the Jewish People, 82, 120
Central Database of Shoah Victims' Names, 94, 96
Centro de Estudios Migratorios Latinoamericanos, 117
Centro di Documentazione Ebraica Contemporanea, 83
Cercle de Généalogie Juive, 64, 118
certificates
    baby-naming, 10
    bar and bat mitzvah, 10, 12
    birth, 9, 12, 40, 85, 123
    brit milah, 12

citizenship, 39
death, 10, 12, 17, 40, 60, 134
    Honorable Discharge, 45
    marriage, 9, 12, 41, 42, 61, 90, 104
    naturalization, 10, 12, 60
charts
    ancestry chart, 7
    descendant chart, 6, 7
    yahrzeit, 11, 12, 125
Christian name. *See* first name
chuppah, 88
Church of Jesus Christ of Latter-day Saints, The, 117
circumcision. *See* brit milah
citizenship
    certificate, 39
    records, 38, 39, 60, 72
city directories, 42, 43, 63
cjhn.ca, 59, 117
cjh.org, 83, 117
Cochin Jews, 83
Collection de cartes postales historiques de la France, 64
commercial directories, 63, 65
concentration camp, 95
Conscriptio Judæorum, 85
Consistoire de Paris, 64, 117
consistoire.org, 64, 117
conversion, 101, 102
Converso Genealogy Project, 101
conversos, 101
coraweb.com.au, 117
county directories, 63
cremation, 57, 58
criminals, 102
Croatia, 63
crypto-Jews, 66, 101, 118. *See also* marranos
Cyprus, 97
Cyrillic, 3, 33, 72, 90, 123
Czech, 20, 22, 83, 115
    Republic, 63, 115
Czechoslovakia, 64, 95

D

Davar, 48
death, 11
    announcements, 47, 48
    cause of, 40
    certificates, 10, 12, 17, 40, 60, 134
    dates, 5, 11, 12, 40, 49, 58, 87
    places, 5, 6
    records, 60, 61, 67, 101, 116, 118, 125
deathindexes.com, 117
Département, 64
derekh-eretsdik, 105
descendant chart, 6, 7
detention of immigrants, 78
dialects, 20, 21, 32, 33
diaries, 44
digitalarchives.bt.com/Calmview, 62, 117

digitization, 108, 109, 110
diplomas, 10, 12
directories
    business, 65, 86
    business, Poland, 86
    Carpathian Ruthenia Business, 1925, 86
    city, 42, 43, 63
    commercial, 63, 65
    county, 63
    Industry and Trade of Hungary, 1891, 86
    professional, 43
    telephone, 42, 66, 99, 102, 120
discs
    archival, 107
divorce, 90, 103, 104, 105
DNA
    autosomal, 16, 123
    mitochondrial, 16, 124
    testing, 15, 16, 17, 123, 124, 125
    Y, 16
documents
    military, 10
    probate, 11, 46
    real estate, 11, 12
    wills, 11, 12
dog tag, 62
double names, 19, 20
Drouin records, 61
Dzhudezmo, 33, 123. *See also* Ladino

E

Eastern Europe, 1, 32, 72, 73, 81, 82, 123, 124
Egypt, 89
Electoral Rolls
    Australian, 61
elector lists, 87, 88
    State Duma, 88
Ellis Island, 17, 69, 71, 72, 73, 76, 77, 78, 79, 121, 123, 134
    name-changing myth, 71, 72
emigration records, 61
England, 21, 59, 60, 63, 70
    General Register Office (GRO), 60
English, 9, 11, 19, 20, 25, 32, 33, 48, 55, 58, 59, 64, 72, 74, 93, 98, 99, 116, 117
Espanyol. *See* Ladino
Estonia, 14
Ethiopian Jews, 23
Europe, 1, 13, 14, 20, 21, 23, 32, 55, 59, 63, 64, 65, 66, 69, 70, 72, 73, 81, 82, 83, 87, 93, 95, 97, 98, 103, 104, 123, 124, 134
Evangelical-Lutheran Parish records, 82

F

Fallen Citizens in the State of Israel, 98
familysearch.org, 38, 40, 42, 44, 65, 71, 83, 86, 88, 107, 117
Family Tree of the Jewish People, 8, 111

farhi.org, 82, 117
Federal Bureau of Investigation (FBI), 103
findagrave.com, 57, 91, 98, 117
First *Aliyah*, 97
FOIA. *See* Freedom of Information Act
foia.gov, 103
fold3.com, 44, 117
foods, 13, 14, 15
Forverts, 48
Fraktur, 34, 35, 134
France, 22, 63, 64, 66, 70, 115, 118
    Guide for the Jewish Traveler, 64
freebmd.org.uk, 118
French, 20, 32, 33, 48, 63, 64, 79, 82, 84, 118
    Jews, 63
    Postal Codes, 64
fultonhistory.com, 48, 118, 134

G

Galitsyaner, 13, 14, 123
GEDCOM, 111
genealogical societies, 59, 61, 98, 112, 116, 118, 119. *See also* genealogy clubs
genealogy
    clubs, 8, 29, 30, 45, 111. *See also* genealogical societies
    conferences, 112, 118
    software, 8, 111
genealogybank.com, 118
genealogyindexer.org/directories, 118
genealogy.org.il, 98, 99, 118
genealoj.org/fr, 64, 118
General Register Office (GRO), 60
Georgia, 14
geresh, 52, 53
German, 20, 22, 23, 32, 34, 35, 48, 64, 72, 76, 79, 82, 83, 84, 93, 115, 125
    Collection, 64, 82
    Jews, 64
    Towns Project, 1933, 83
Germanic languages, 32
Germany, 22, 34, 35, 48, 63, 64, 70, 82, 85, 95
Gesher Galicia, 63
geshergalicia.org, 63, 84, 118
get, 105
gfh.org.il/eng, 98, 118
Ghetto Fighters' House Museum, 98, 118
Gibraltar, 23, 115
Grand Trunk Railway, 69
gravestones, 31, 44, 49, 50, 51, 53, 54, 55, 57, 58, 89, 98, 117, 119, 124
    mistakes, 50
    symbols, 49, 50
Greece, 1, 33, 63, 82
Greek
    alphabet, 33
    Jews, 23, 82
GRO. *See* General Register Office (GRO)
gro.gov.uk, 60, 118
groom, 13, 88, 89, 90

gubernia, 81, 82, 85, 88, 123, 134
guides.loc.gov, 42, 118

H

Haganah Historical Archives, 98
Haggadah, 1, 21, 31, 32, 33
Haketia. *See* Ladino
HaMelitz, 48, 134
Hanukkah, 11, 13, 50
Har HaZeitim, 98
hebcal.com, 53, 118
Hebrew, 94
    alphabet, 1, 3, 31, 32, 33, 50, 51, 52, 53, 99
    calendar, 51, 53
    dates, 49, 51, 58, 88, 89
    language, 20, 21, 22, 23, 31, 32, 49, 50, 51, 53, 54, 55, 65, 66, 84, 97, 98, 99
    months, 53
    names, 19, 21, 43, 55, 73
    numerals, 52
Hebrew Sick Benefit Association, 62
help.nytimes.com, 48
Hesse-Nassau Civil Records and Church Books, 82
High Priests. *See* Kohanim
Historical Jewish Press, 90
Hoffman, William F., 116
Holocaust, 32, 59, 64, 65, 93, 94, 95, 96, 99, 105, 112, 121, 122, 124, 125
    Survivors and Victims Database, 95
Honorable Discharge certificate, 45
Hungary, 13, 14, 63, 64, 65, 81, 82, 84, 85, 86, 95, 118
    Database, 65
    Industry and Trade Directory of, 1891, 86
    National Archives of, 65

I

iajgscemetery.org, 98, 118
iajgs.org, 112, 118
Iberian Peninsula, 23
Identity Card, 62
ijarchive.org, 85, 118
image-processing software, 108
indexes
    birth, 61, 64, 65
    marriage, 41, 42
    Social Security Applications and Claims, 46
    United States Social Security Death (SSDI), 46
India, 83
Industry and Trade Directory of Hungary, 1891, 86
instituteofjewishexperience.org/ancestral-search/, 118
International
    Association of Jewish ies (IAJGS), 98, 112, 118

Jewish Cemetery Project, 98
    Tracing Service (ITS), 95
Internet Archive, 86
interviews, 8, 15, 95, 98, 121
invitations, 11, 12, 13
    wedding, 13
Iraqi
    Jews, 118
    Mukharabat Archive of Jewish Materials, 118
Ireland, Republic of, 60
Israel, 1, 23, 48, 59, 63, 65, 66, 83, 94, 97, 98, 99, 105, 118, 119, 120, 123
    Defense Force, 98
    Genealogy Research Association (IGRA), 98
    National Library of, 99, 120
    Phone Book, 99
Israeli Association for the Study of Family Roots, 99, 119
israelpb.com, 99, 119
isragen.org.il, 99, 119
Italian, 22, 33, 119
    Genealogical Group, 119
    Jews, 23
italian-family-history.com/jewish/genealogy.html, 83, 119
italiangen.org, 42, 58, 119
Italy, 63, 70, 83, 115, 119
izkor.gov.il, 98, 119

J

Jeff Malka Sephardic Collection, 82
Jewish
    calendar, 118. *See also* Hebrew calendar
    colonies, 66
    Colonization Association, 66
    Communities and Records - United Kingdom Database, 59
    Genealogical Society, Australian, 61, 116
    Genealogical Society of Montréal, 59, 61, 119
    Genealogy Family Finder, 111
    Heritage Network, Canadian, 59, 61, 117
    languages, 31, 32, 33
    months, 53
    names, 5, 6, 8, 9, 10, 11, 19, 25, 26, 27, 29, 31, 49, 50, 51, 55, 58, 72, 77, 88, 89, 90
    National Fund, 97
    newspapers, 48
    Records Indexing—Poland, 63
    star, 50. *See also* magen david
    year, 53
JewishGen, 82, 85, 98, 111, 119, 133
    Germany Database, 82
    Online Worldwide Burial Registry (JOWBR), 57, 91, 98, 119
jewishgen.org, 8, 48, 57, 64, 65, 66, 82, 83, 86, 88, 91, 94, 96, 98, 99, 111, 116, 119
    Discussion Group, 111
JewishGen Press, 94, 96, 133
jewishroots.uct.ac.za, 59, 119
jewishturkstones.tau.ac.il, 91, 119
jgs-montreal.org, 59, 119
j-italy.org, 119
jnf.org/our-work/heritage-site-preservation, 98
JOWBR, 57, 91
JRI–Poland, 85
jri-poland.org, 63, 84, 85, 86, 119
Judeo-Espagnol. *See* Ladino

K

kahal records, 83, 88
kehilalinks.jewishgen.org, 66
Keneder Adler, 62
ketubot, 9, 12, 31, 32, 42, 53, 88, 89, 90, 105, 124
Khurbn. *See* Holocaust
kinnui, 19
kipot, 9, 12. *See also* skull caps, yarmulkes
Kohanim, 11, 16, 22, 49, 50, 51, 54, 88, 89, 90, 124
Kohen Tzedek, 22
Kurrent, 34, 35

L

laad.btl.gov.il, 98, 119
Ladino, 2, 33, 67, 123, 134
LaKarov v'Larahok, 99
landsmanshaftn, 55, 56, 94, 124
last names. *See* surnames
Latin, 34, 55, 66, 81, 85
Latvia, 14, 70
Les Fleurs de l'Orient, 82, 117
letters, 10, 12, 31, 32, 44
Levi'im, 22, 49, 54, 88, 89, 90, 124
Liberté, La, 48
libguides.nypl.org/yizkorbooks, 94
Library and Archives Canada, 60, 120, 121
library-archives.canada.ca, 60, 120
Library of Congress, 42, 86, 118, 120
licenses
    marriage, 47
lists
    electors, 87, 88
    merchants, 88
    Rabbi's Elector, 88
    voter, 61, 65
Lithuania, 14, 22, 48, 85, 87, 115, 120
    Tax and Voters Lists for, 1846, 87
Litvaks, 14, 21, 59, 115, 120, 124
litvaksig.org, 120
Litvak Special Interest Group, 120
loc.gov/rr/european/tel.html, 86, 120
Lorraine, 64
Luxembourg, 63

M

Macedon, 19
magazine articles, 11
magen david, 50
maiden names, 46
Malka, Jeffrey S., 67, 82, 85, 115
maps, 11, 65
    cemeteries, 11, 12, 58
marranos, 66, 101. *See also* crypto-Jews
marriage, 5
    certificates, 9, 12, 41, 42, 61, 90, 104
    contracts. *See ketubot*
    indexes, 41, 42
    licenses, 47
    multiple, 103, 104
    records, 61, 67, 84, 85, 99
matzeva. *See* gravestones
medals, 10, 12, 44, 62
    military, 10, 90
medical registers, 63
Memorial of the Shoah, 64
Menk, Lars, 115
menorahs, 11, 50
Merchant Lists, 88
Mexico, 66, 67, 69
microfilms, 70
military
    documents, 10
    medals, 10, 62, 90
    records, 44, 61, 90, 91, 98, 117
Miriam Weiner Routes to Roots Foundation, 121
mitochondrial DNA, 16, 124
mitzvah, 3, 30
mitzvatemet.com/en/burials, 57, 91, 120
Mizrahi Jews, 22
mnl.gov.hu, 65
Moldova Republic, 66
Moroccan Jews, 66
Morocco, 48, 90
Morse, Steve, 73, 121, 131
movies, 109
multiple marriages, 103, 104
mutual aid societies, 55, 56
myheritage.com, 38, 42, 44, 65, 67, 71, 83, 88, 120

N

naa.gov.au, 60, 120
name-changing, 99
    myth at Ellis Island, 71, 72
names
    ancient, 19
    Arabic, 19
    double, 19, 20
    Hebrew, 19, 21, 43, 55, 73
    Jewish, 5, 6, 8, 19, 25, 26, 27, 29, 31, 49, 50, 51, 55, 58, 72, 77, 88, 89, 90
    maiden, 46
    nicknames, 20, 25
    patronymics, 21, 86
    secular, 19, 20, 25, 88
    surnames, 21
    talmudic, 19
naming customs, 20, 22, 23
NARA, 39, 116
National
    Archives and Records Administration (NARA), 38, 116
    Archives of Australia, 60, 120
    Archives of Hungary, 65
    Jewish Welfare Board, 44
    Library of Israel, 99, 120
nationalarchives.gov.uk, 60, 120
nationalarchives.gov.za, 60, 120
naturalization, 10, 12, 38, 39, 40, 60, 124
    Certificates of, 10, 12, 60
    Petition for, 39, 40
    records, 38, 60, 82
Nazis, 34, 35, 64, 66, 93
negatives, 109
New Christians, 101. *See also* conversos, marranos, crypto-Jews
newspaperarchive.com, 120
newspaper articles, 10, 12, 13, 32, 44, 47, 58, 102, 120
newspapers
    Amérika, La, 48
    Aufbau, 48
    Brooklyn Eagle, 117
    Davar, 48
    Forverts, 48
    HaMelitz, 48, 134
    Keneder Adler, 62
    LaKarov v'Larahok, 99
    Liberté, La, 48
    New York Times, 121
    Occident and American Jewish Advocate, 48
    OJCZYZNA, 48
    Standard Union, 47, 134
newspapers.com, 120
New York Public Library, 33, 94, 120
New York Times, 121
nicknames, 20, 25
nli.org.il, 48, 82, 90, 99, 120, 134
North African Jews, 14, 66
North America, 1, 43, 69, 102, 104, 134
Northern Ireland, 60
nypl.org, 94, 120, 134

O

obd-memorial.ru/html, 90, 120
obituaries, 10, 47, 48, 62
Occident and American Jewish Advocate, 48
OJCZYZNA, 48
onlysimchas.com, 120
Ottoman Empire, 33, 66, 82, 88, 97, 119

P

pages
    archival, 108, 109
    of Testimony, 94, 96, 112, 124, 134
pair of hands symbol, 50
Pale of Settlement, 81, 82, 124
Palestine, 31, 97, 98, 99, 116
paper sleeves
    archival, 110
Paratroops Heritage Association, The, 98
paratroops.org.il, 98, 120
Passover, 1, 14, 19, 21, 31, 32, 33, 53
passports, 10, 29, 78, 79, 80, 99, 124
patents, 47
patents.google.com, 47, 120
patronymics, 21, 86
pedigree collapse, 29, 103
Persia, 82
Petition for Naturalization, 39, 40
phonograph records, 110
photo albums, 44
photographs, 10, 12, 13, 44, 54, 108
pitcher, 54
pogroms, 66
Poland, 14, 17, 22, 48, 56, 63, 64, 81, 82, 85, 86, 97, 99, 111, 115, 119
    State Archives, 85
Polish, 20, 22, 33, 48, 66, 72, 76, 82, 84, 85, 86, 91, 97
    Business Directories, 86
    Jews, 66
    State Archives, 85
Polish State Archives, 63, 85, 116
ports, 70, 71, 78
    of departure, 71
    of emigration, 70
    of entry, 69, 123
Portugal, 20, 23, 33, 66, 82, 125
Portuguese, 22, 115
Posen, 22, 64
postcards, 2, 10, 12, 13, 64, 67, 118
prayer books. *See siddurim*
probate, 11, 46
    documents, 11
professional directories, 43
p'tur, 105

R

R', 50, 51
Rabbi's Elector lists, 88
Rashi script, 33
readcoop.eu/transkribus/, 120
real estate
    documents, 11, 12
    records, 87
Reb, 51
recherche-collection-search.bac-lac.gc.ca/eng/Census/Index, 121
Reclaim the Records, 121
reclaimtherecords.org, 121
recordings
    audio, 8, 9, 10, 12, 107, 109
    video, 8, 10, 12
recording sources, 17

records
- birth, 61, 65, 67, 85, 99, 134
- border crossing, 67, 77
- census, 37, 38, 60, 85
- citizenship, 38, 60
- death, 60, 61, 67, 85, 99, 101, 116, 118, 125
- Drouin, 61
- emigration, 61
- Evangelical-Lutheran Parish, 82
- *kahal*, 83, 88
- marriage, 61, 67, 84, 85, 99
- military, 44, 61, 90, 91, 98, 117
- naturalization, 38, 60, 82
- photograph, 110
- real estate, 87
- tax, 86, 88
- vinyl, 110
- voter, 86, 88

Roman
- alphabet, 33, 72
- Empire, 19, 63
- numerals, 51, 52

Romance language, 33
Romania, 1, 13, 63, 93
Romaniote Jews, 82
Rosenstein, Neil, 115
Rosin, Josef, 115
Routes to Roots Foundation, 85, 121
rtrfoundation.org, 85, 121
Russia, 14, 20, 66, 72, 75, 79, 81, 82, 85, 86, 87, 88, 90, 103, 104, 134
- All-Russia Census of 1858, 85

Russian
- alphabet, 3, 21, 33, 34. *See also* Cyrillic
- Empire, 21, 33, 34, 65, 72, 73, 77, 79, 81, 82, 85, 88, 90, 102, 115, 123, 124
- Jews, 66
- language, 2, 20, 22, 23, 33, 34, 48, 65, 66, 79, 80, 84, 87, 90, 120, 123
- Poland, 81
- Revolution, 34, 66

Russian-Jewish Fallen Soldiers of WWI, 65

S

Saint Cyril, 33
Sammlung historischer Postkarten aus Deutschland und Österreich, 64
Scotland, 60
scrapbooks, 44
secular names, 9, 11, 19, 20, 25, 88
Seder, 1
Semitic languages, 31
Sephardic Collection, 61, 82
sephardicgen.com, 67, 85, 121
Sephardim, 14, 20, 21, 22, 23, 33, 55, 59, 66, 82, 83, 85, 88, 98, 115, 117, 118, 119, 121, 123
Serbia, 63
sfi.usc.edu, 95, 121
Shabbat candles, 87, 110

Shavuot, 14
Shea, Jonathan D., 116
shem hakodesh, 19
shidekh, 29
ship manifest, 70, 71, 72, 76, 79, 98, 125, 134
Shoah. *See* Holocaust
- Survivors and Refugees Registration Forms, 94
- Victims' Names Recovery Project, 94

Shown Mills, Elizabeth, 115
shtetls, 1, 56, 82, 103, 119
siddurim, 11
SIGs. *See* Special Interest Groups
Silesia, 64
skull caps, 9. *See also* yarmulkes, *kipot*
Slavic languages, 22, 23, 32, 33
slides, 109
Social Security, 46, 125
- Administration, 46, 125
- Applications and Claims Index, 46
- Death Index, United States (SSDI), 46
- records, 46

Society for Preservation of Israel Heritage Sites, 97
software
- genealogy, 8, 111

Solitreo, 33
South Africa, 59, 60, 61
South African
- Jewish Rootsbank, 60, 61, 119
- Jews, 61

souvenirs, 10, 11, 12
Soviet Union, 11, 33, 65, 88, 90, 120
Spain, 20, 23, 33, 63, 66, 82, 101, 125
Spanish, 20, 22, 33, 66, 101, 117, 123
- Inquisition, 66

Special Interest Groups, 84
spelling, 72, 77
SSDI, 46
Standard Union, 47, 134
State Duma electors lists, 88
statueofliberty.org, 71, 76, 121
stevemorse.org, 71, 73, 121
Steve Morse's One-Step Webpages, 73, 121
storage pages, 107, 108, 109
surnames, 21, 65, 72
Sütterlin, 34, 35
Switzerland, 63, 64
symbols on gravestones, 49, 50, 54, 58
- book, 54
- carvings of animals, 54
- *magen david*, 50
- menorah, 50
- pair of hands, 50
- pitcher, 54
- tree stump, 54

Syria, 66
Syriac, 32

T

Table décennale, 64

Tagger, Mathilde A., 115
tahrir defterleri, 88
tallitot, 11
Talmud, 19, 21, 101
talmudic names, 19
tax
- and Voters Lists for Lithuania, 1846, 87
- records, 86, 87, 88

telephone books. *See* telephone directories
telephone directories, 42, 43, 62, 66, 86, 99, 102, 116, 120
telexplorer.com.ar, 66
The Joint, 82
timesmachine.nytimes.com/browser, 121
Tolerance Taxes, 85
Torah, 19, 21, 31, 38, 97, 101, 104
Town Finder, 94
traits, 1, 5
Transkribus, 120
tree stump, 54
T'udat-Aliya, 97
Tunisia, 64
Turkey, 14, 88, 90, 119
Turkish, 33, 88, 97, 121
- Cultural Foundation, 88, 121

turkishculture.org, 88, 121

U

ukcensusonline.com, 121
Ukraine, 13, 54, 56, 63, 65, 66, 84, 85, 86, 93, 95, 115
- Database, 65

Ukrainian, 22, 23, 33, 65, 84, 90, 121, 123, 134
uk.wikisource.org/wiki/Архів:Єврейське_містечко, 65, 121
United Kingdom, 59, 60, 61, 62, 63, 118, 121
- Database, 59, 61

United States, 10, 11, 14, 20, 37, 38, 39, 40, 43, 44, 45, 46, 51, 56, 59, 60, 61, 62, 63, 64, 65, 66, 67, 69, 71, 72, 73, 75, 77, 78, 82, 86, 95, 99, 102, 103, 104, 111, 116, 117, 118, 120, 121, 123, 125
- Citizenship and Immigration Services (USCIS), 72
- Consular Records, 99
- Federal Bureau of Investigation (FBI), 103
- Federal Census, 37, 38, 103
- Holocaust Memorial Museum, 95
- Library of Congress, 86, 120
- National Archives and Records Administration (NARA), 38, 116
- Social Security Death Index (SSDI), 46
- State Census, 38

USC Shoah Foundation – The Institute for Visual History and Education, 95
ushmm.org, 95, 99, 121

V

veterans, 44

video recordings, 8, 10, 12
videotapes, 109
vinyl records, 110
visas, 71, 72
voter
    lists, 61, 65
    records, 86, 88

W

Wales, 60
weddings, 9, 11, 13
    announcements, 47, 48
wills, 11, 12
wine cups, 11, 13, 110
worldjewishtravel.org, 64
World War I, 10, 44, 45, 81, 82, 97, 124
    Draft Registration Cards, 44
World War II, 34, 44, 45, 62, 64, 65, 69, 82, 85, 86, 90, 93, 95, 98, 101, 123
    Draft Registration Cards, 44

Y

Yad Vashem, 94, 95, 96, 112, 124, 134
yadvashem.org, 95, 112, 122, 134
yahrzeit, 11, 12, 125
    charts, 11, 12, 125
yarmulkes, 9, 12. *See also* skull caps, *kipot*
Y-DNA, 16
yearbooks, 10, 12, 43
Yemenite Jews, 23
Yiddish, 2, 9, 13, 14, 20, 21, 22, 23, 29, 32, 33, 43, 48, 54, 55, 62, 66, 69, 71, 72, 73, 74, 77, 87, 90, 93, 94, 99, 105, 123, 124, 125, 133, 134
Yiddish Book Center, 94
yiddishbookcenter.org/collections/yizkor-books, 94, 122
yivo.org, 122
Yizkor Book Project, 94
Yizkor Books, 32, 64, 65, 93, 94, 95, 118, 119, 120, 122, 125
Yugntruf—Youth for Yiddish, 32

About the authors

CARYN ALTER, a registered dietitian by profession, started her genealogy journey in college, when she mailed family history questionnaires to her relatives (She still has all their responses!). Caryn, who also has a background in journalism, has written articles and feature stories for newspapers and magazines on various topics, including food and nutrition. She has done genealogy presentations throughout New Jersey and surrounding areas, and has a special interest in researching the clues that Jewish food traditions can provide regarding one's Jewish heritage. Caryn has been a singer in Jewish choirs for many years.

STEPHEN M. COHEN began his genealogy quest as part of a second-grade school project. (Really!) He has a Ph.D. in chemistry, is a Board Member of the Midwest Jewish Studies Association, and is a writer and lecturer on many topics, both chemical and Jewish. His published books include *America's Scientific Treasures*, 2nd edition (Oxford University Press) and *O Mg! How Chemistry Came to Be* (World Scientific). He is a professional Judaic calligrapher, a published choral composer, and raised his two adult children to be native Yiddish speakers. He is the creator and host of the popular *The History of Chemistry* podcast.

BOTH AUTHORS, who helped found the Mercer County Jewish Genealogy Society at Beth El Synagogue, would be happy to give presentations (in-person or virtual) on various aspects of Jewish genealogy to your organization. You can reach them through JewishGen Press or at **WhatsInaName.JewishGen@gmail.com**.

Image Credits

pp. xix, 16 Magnifying glass: from https://upload.wikimedia.org/wikipedia/commons/8/80/Magnifying_glass.jpg. Modified the image by Tomomarusan via a Creative Commons license.

p. 5 Red-haired girl: Photo by Jennifer Burk on Unsplash.

p. 16 Diagram of DNA: from https://upload.wikimedia.org/wikipedia/commons/thumb/e/e7/DNA_simple.svg/2000px-DNA_simple.svg.png. Used with Creative Commons license.

p. 31 Hebrew text: Meir Halevi Letteris, *Megilat Ester (Story of Esther)*, Hebrew Publishing Company, New York, n.d., p. 1189.

p. 32 Yiddish text: Dr. Ab. Caspe, *Geologye, Tsveyte Teyl: Taykhn un Shtromen*, Arbeter-Ring Bibliotek num. XI, New York, N.Y.: Edyukeyshonal Komite Arbeter-Ring, 1918, p. 54.

p. 33 Ladino *Robinson Crusoe*: from https://digitalcollections.nypl.org/items/cf94e390-236b-0138-cb3f-3d22a2e514d9.

p. 34 Fraktur: Friedrich von Schiller, *Wilhelm Tell: Schauspiel in fünf Auszügen*, ed. Wiliam Dwight Whitney, New York, N.Y.: Henry Holt and Company, New York, 1877, p. 98–99.

p. 43 Yearbook photograph: *The Seal*, Trenton State College, Ewing, New Jersey, 1966, p. 15.

p. 47 "Vacation Personals" column: from https://fultonhistory.com/Fulton.html. *Brooklyn Standard Union*, Sep. 4, 1921, p. B7.

p. 48 *HaMelitz* notice: from https://www.nli.org.il/en/newspapers/hmz/1899/04/18/01/page/7/?e=-------en-20--1--img-tx-IN%7ctxTI--------------1. *HaMelitz*, April 18, 1899, p. 7.

p. 60 British death certificate reproduced with the permission of the Controller of Her Majesty's Stationery Office. © Crown copyright 2016.

p. 65 Ukrainian Jewish birth records from 1878: from https://uk.wikisource.org/wiki/Архів:ДАЖО/67/3/462. Photography by Alexander Krakovsky/CC BY-SA 4.0.

p. 69 Map of North America: Created using the map by Gringer at https://upload.wikimedia.org/wikipedia/commons/thumb/a/ae/aunion.svg/2000px-Naunion.svg.png under the terms of the Creative Commons Attribution-Share Alike 2.5 Generic license, found at https://creativecommons.org/licenses/by-sa/2.5/deed.en.

p. 70 Map of Europe: Created using the map found at https://en.wikipedia.org/wiki/Europe#/media/File:Blank_map_of_Europe_(polar_stereographic_projection)_cropped.svg under the terms of the GNU Free Documentation License found at https://commons.wikimedia.org/wiki/Commons:GNU_Free_Documentation_License,_version_1.2.

pp. 70, 76 1910 Ellis Island ship manifest: Photo courtesy of the Statue of Liberty—Ellis Island Foundation, www.libertyellisfoundation.org.

p. 79 1914 Ellis Island ship manifest: Photo courtesy of the Statue of Liberty—Ellis Island Foundation, www.libertyellisfoundation.org.

p. 81 Map of Gubernias: Modified from Herman Rosenthal, J.G. Lipman, Vasili Rosenthal, L. Wygodsky; M. Mysh, Abraham Galante (1905), "Russia" in *The Jewish Encyclopedia*, Vol. X, Philipson–Samoscz, New York, N.Y.: Funk & Wagnalls, 1905, p. 531.

p. 83 Map of the Mediterranean: https://commons.wikimedia.org/wiki/File:Mediterranean_Sea_location_map.svg By NordNordWest - Own work using World Data Base II data, CC BY-SA 3.0, https://commons.wikimedia.org/w/index.php?curid=11416503.

p. 94 Page of Testimony: from https://collections.yadvashem.org/en/names, courtesy of THE CENTRAL DATABASE OF SHOAH VICTIMS' NAMES, Yad Vashem.

p. 95 Personal Card File: from https://collections.yadvashem.org/en/names, courtesy of THE CENTRAL DATABASE OF SHOAH VICTIMS' NAMES, Yad Vashem.

Trademark notice: Kodachrome is a registered trademark of The Eastman Kodak Company.

www.ingramcontent.com/pod-product-compliance
Lightning Source LLC
Chambersburg PA
CBHW080746250426
43673CB00062B/1926